AALIYAH AND TROY

A feature film screen play by:
Mike Messier & Aaron Woodson

Inspired by the books
THE FACE OF EXPRESSION
and
THE FACE OF EXPRESSION TWO: IN YOUR FACE
By Aaron Woodson

AALIYAH and TROY
© June 2021 by Mike Messier and Aaron Woodson

ISBN# 978-1-953526-17-5

Mike Messier
424-386-1038
mikemessiermoviemaker@gmail.com
www.mikemessier.com

Aaron Woodson
904-237-2582
awoodson24hbl@gmail.com

All rights reserved under international copyright law. This book or parts of thereof may not be reproduced in any form, stored in a retrieval system, or transmitted in any form by any means; electronic, mechanical, photocopy, recording, or otherwise without prior written permission of the publisher or author, except as provided by United States of America copyright.

Published by TaylorMade Publishing
Jacksonville, FL
www.TaylorMadePublishingFL.com
(904) 323-1334

TaylorMade Publishing

Introduction

Troy is a good man who suffers from PTSD complications after serving time in the military overseas. He is at his favorite morning coffee house checking the help wanted ads, when he meets an attractive gym instructor coming out of work named Aaliyah. They start a conversation which eventually goes off the tracks when Troy brings up his Christian beliefs.

A few days later, Troy is back at the coffee house, where he accidentally bumps into Rosa, a young girl, nine years old, and Rosa's coffee spills on the floor. Troy helps clean up the mess and it is revealed that Rosa is, in fact, Aaliyah 's daughter. Aaliyah and Troy give their friendship a second chance and hit it off much better, including a brief kiss.

Troy sees this as an indicator he has found "the one" but Aaliyah pulls back. This causes Troy frustration that he shares with his Veterans Support Group. Aaliyah invites Troy to "Club Expressions", a spoken word / poetry hipster club that her sister Monica manages. Initially feeling out of place by the hipsters with dyed hair and pierced body parts and the offerings of kombucha, Troy has an awkward confrontation with poet Heckler J in front of the club. Using his natural good will, Troy is able to talk the situation down in a classy way, making his presence known to the club members as a good guy and a new creative force on the scene.

As such, Troy is invited by Aaliyah 's meddling sister Monica to compete in the poetry slam competition the next week. What Monica didn't tell Troy is that Aaliyah 's "baby daddy" Brett, who Monica doesn't especially care for herself, is the returning poetry champion who will also be competing in the poetry tournament. Aaliyah herself will also be competing in the tournament.

Somehow, Troy has found himself in a "love triangle" that he wasn't expecting, and his emotions are now wrangled up way beyond his comfort level, pushing him further to the edge. Further complicating Troy 's life are his quest for a full-time job and his memberships in a Veteran Supports Group and a Church prayer group, both of which aim to help him with his struggles with PTSD.

Not seeing much hope in a relationship with Aaliyah, despite his best efforts, Troy nonetheless forces himself to compete in the poetry tournament, if not to prove something to Aaliyah, at least to himself.

FADE IN:

EXT. COFFEE HOUSE – day

Troy, 35, African-American, approaches his usual coffee house on foot, with a huge Sunday newspaper under his arm. He slows his pace when he notices a DOG, which does not have any owner nearby and is not wearing a leash, standing nearby the coffee house entrance like a self-appointed singular gargoyle. The dog is of a breed that nearly resembles a wolf.

Troy does not stop walking towards the coffee house, he eyes the dog and the dog eyes Troy. A sense of respect. No need to pet. No need to bark. Troy passes by the dog and enters the coffee house.

INT. COFFEE HOUSE – DAY

The coffee house owner, Slava, 60, Bosnian, a hospitable, cocktail story of a man, with a zest for over-the-top humor, greets Troy.

> **SLAVA:**
> These strays, man. They got nowhere to go.

> **TROY:**
> You saw him? He doesn't belong to anybody?

Slava whacks TROY: on the back.

> **SLAVA:**
> I'm talking about you. Now find a job, so you start paying off your bill. It's getting close to the three digits, man.

Moments later, Troy sits at a table by himself, glancing at his coffee and the classifieds section of the Sunday paper. He has several "Help

Wanted" ads circled and some crossed out with his red sharpie magic marker.

Troy also has a bunch of notes scrawled on the side of the ads.

Troy pulls something out of his pocket and looks at it. From our perspective, we can tell it's about the size of a half-dollar, but we can't see what it is for sure.

> **TROY:** (under his breath, to himself)
> One day at a time.

Troy's eyes look up just as a beautiful young woman, Aaliyah, comes in. She's about 27, athletic, very striking, and dressed in form fitting gym attire.

She catches him looking her over and gives him a pointed look as if to admonish him for staring. Troy puts the object back into his pocket quickly.

Troy smiles as if confessing that he's been busted. She just shakes her head slightly. At this point, he's forced to make his move. TROY: stands and approaches her

> **TROY:** (Cont'd):
> Uh, you just came from the gym?
>
> **AALIYAH::**
> So, you're a rocket scientist?
>
> **TROY:**
> Uhm...
>
> **AALIYAH:**
> You make rockets, right? I mean, to figure it out? The gym's across the parking lot and I'm in here

wearing my spanx. So, as a rocket scientist you could figure out that I just got outta the gym. Look at you.

TROY:
Well, yes. By my calculations, you are 1,000 years into the future of technology... between your spanx, how you fill them out and that coffee of yours I'm about to have Slava put on my bill, you are well ahead of the game.

AALIYAH:
The game, huh?

EXT. PARK - DAY

Troy and Aaliyah, now walk close by each other through the otherwise abandoned park, both with "to go" cups from the Coffee House.

AALIYAH:
So, game player, you from around here?

TROY:
Nah. I'm from Cali... you ever been?

AALIYAH:
I wish. Why don't you take me there?

TROY:
You got some money to put in on this? Flying doesn't come cheap!

AALIYAH:
Boy, please! I'm independent, I can pay my own way. I don't need a man for all that.

Aaliyah walks over a small rock, causing her to almost trip.

> **TROY:**
> You okay?

> **AALIYAH:**
> This damn shoe. Doesn't fit right.

Troy points to a nearby bench.

> **TROY:**
> Sit down. Let the doctor fix it.

> **AALIYAH:** (taken aback)
> Okay, then.

Aaliyah goes to the bench and sits down. Troy drops to one knee in front of her.

> **AALIYAH:** (cont'd)
> Wait, you fixin' to bust out a ring or somethin'?
>
> She gestures as if there are hidden TV cameras in the park.
>
> **AALIYAH:** (Cont'd)
> Where's the cameras at? Hello?!

> **TROY:**
> Okay, okay, let me see.

He slips off one of her shoes and inspects it.
> **TROY:** (Cont'd)
> Okay, this one looks all right.

AALIYAH:
My foot?

TROY:
Your shoe. But this other one?

Troy snaps his fingers to get her to lift up her another foot. She shakes her head but does it anyway.

TROY: (Cont'd)
You can trust me. I was the boot 'n' shoe expert in my company. They called me 'Soldier Scholl'.

AALIYAH:
Ten-hut then, soldier.

Troy takes off her other shoe off her foot. Then he uses his fingers to unofficially measure both of her feet, going back and forth between them.

AALIYAH: (Cont'd)
Hey, that tickles.

TROY:
Just as I suspected. You're an off-size.

AALIYAH:
Off what?

TROY:
What are you? A nine? An eight?

AALIYAH: (initially lying then correcting herself out of guilt)
A seven. An eight. Eight and a half.

TROY:
Okay, Miss Eight and a half. You find it hard to buy shoes? Can't ever get an exact fit?

AALIYAH:
(defensive) Yeah. So?

TROY:
That's 'cause one of your 'eight and a halfs' is more like a nine and the other one is more like an eight.

AALIYAH:
Really?

TROY:
Yeah. So, you got one foot struggling to be in these shoes and other one is loose as a goose in there.

AALIYAH:
Loose as a damn goose, huh?

TROY:
And this doesn't help either.

Troy turns one of her shoes upside down, taps it on the toe and a bunch of dirt falls out of it.

Aaliyah blushes a bit.

AALIYAH:
My word...

TROY:
Sometimes our shoes are filled with sand and it gradually starts to slow us down. Blisters and

calluses can take form when things rub us the wrong way.

AALIYAH:
I ain't got no nasty blisters and calluses; my feet are clean!

TROY:
But you're wearing the wrong size. Es. You're a nine and an eight trying to force yourself to be two 'eights and a halves'.

AALIYAH:
Well, what you do you suppose I do about it, Soldier Scholl? I can't afford to buy two pairs of shoes every time I need new kicks.

TROY:
Find yourself a friend who's got your same problem but with the opposite size feet. Then, you two can buy two pairs of shoes together, one an eight and one a nine, and split 'em up every time.

AALIYAH:
My word. You're too much. I might have to let you buy me a real drink some time.

TROY:
Coffee is a real enough drink for me, my dear.

AALIYAH:
Umm... hmm. What planet did you come from, Troy?

With that question, Troy takes on a different tone. He stands up, looking over Aaliyah for a moment. She looks up to him, confused.

AALIYAH: (Cont'd)
You ain't gonna kill me, are you?

He sits down next to her and lets out a deep breath.

TROY:
I'm a stranger here on Earth but I'm related to the struggle like it was my brother. Ever since birth, I've had to endure a beautiful struggle. My mother strained every last ounce of energy during labor for me to arrive. As a I grew, it became a struggle for me to take my first steps. I stumbled and fell a few times, but I kept getting up and trying again. My lips would quiver and hesitate to speak its first words. Although I stuttered, I somehow managed to get my point across. My little hands were quite slippery as I tried to catch or grab hold of something. Often times, I struggled to listen as a result of my short attention span. As I got older, I struggled with my approach to the opposite sex.

Enduring sacrifice overshadowed my happiness like a dark cloud covering the sun. When I became mature, I gained wisdom through each trial and tribulation.

However, all I was searching for was a father and I found him in Jesus Christ. Through realization, I came to the conclusion it wasn't easy to walk with Jesus. I struggled with faith as if I was balancing on a tight rope without a net. Yet He was with me all the way through that treacherous walk.

Jesus was the net. Your struggle and my struggle look at each other in the same mirror. It reflects how beautiful our struggle really is.

Troy stops talking, proud of himself. Aaliyah soaks in what he just said.

Troy moves in a bit as if to expect a kiss. He closes his eyes.

He hears the sounds of shuffling feet. Troy opens his eyes to see Aaliyah running away from him and out of the park.

We go to Aaliyah, many yards off by now, running and speaking to herself.

AALIYAH:
Another freak. I shoulda known.

Back to Troy on the bench, frustrated at how it all went down, who slumps into the bench, dejected.

INT. COFFEE HOUSE - DAY

Montage of five consecutive mornings. Troy is in different outfits each day and different customers circulate the coffee house each day.

Troy again sits, same spot, now with the classifieds section of the Monday newspaper. He looks up several times, hoping to see Aaliyah but she never enters.

The next day, Tuesday, Troy now with Tuesday's paper, and classifieds section. Out of the corner of his eye, Troy turns his attention to outside.

- INSERT SHOT -

EXT. COFFEE HOUSE - DAY

Troy's POV: Alliyah in an SUV. Sensing Troy seeing her, she backs out of the parking lot in a panic, having never entered the coffee house.

INT. COFFE HOUSE - DAY

Troy shakes his head in disbelief at this.

Cut to Wednesday, Troy again with the Wednesday classifieds, still circling ads. He picks up his smart phone to make a call.

As Troy is on the phone, he notices an eight-year-old girl, Rosa, enter the coffee house on her own.

> **TROY**: (on phone)
> Hello? Hello, Mr. Robinson? Yes, yes, this is Troy. Troy Wilson. Well, I had responded to your help wanted ad for your new restaurant Smokey's opening up on the East Side last week via email and I figured I'd follow up with a phone call. No, I'm not a dishwasher. I'm a chef. A very good one. Well, no, I can be 'just a cook', that doesn't bother me. Whatever you need.

While speaking, Troy notices young Rosa approaches the counter and order two coffees on her own. Troy is perplexed why such a young kid is ordering coffees.

> **TROY**: (Cont'd)
> Okay, yes sir, I'd be happy to stop by anytime and introduce myself in person. I could even cook up a little something for you to show you what I'm capable of. Next month? The first of the month? You sure you need me to wait that long? Okay. I'll be there, Mr. Robinson. And you can call me back at this number if you need me to come in earlier. That's right, that's my number. Thank you.

TROY:
Puts down the phone, a smile crosses his face.
(to himself) Well, it's a start.

TROY: (raises a toast with his coffee to himself.
Here's to me, I guess.

The little girl passes by him and sees his toast.

ROSA:
Here's to you!

Rosa raises a toast with one of her coffee cups to Troy, then she exits. Troy breaks into a laugh.

Thursday, Troy sits again with the classified section but also today with a book, "The Modern Man's Guide to Self-Improvement".

Troy flips through the book. He gets deep into a particular section of it.

TROY: (reading out loud to himself)
There are four seasons that we're fortunate to experience throughout the year. Unfortunately, we don't get the luxury to order the weather that we have... it's already been decided to us. Using visual manifestation, we can predict how the weather patterns will affect our lives.

Troy closes his eyes and takes a deep breath to visualize his energy. He opens his eyes and sees the little girl Rosa from the day before staring at him.

ROSA:
Are you a 'modern man', mister?

TROY:
I try to be, little lady. And let me ask you... how come you're drinking coffee at such a young age? What are you, ten? Eleven?

ROSA:
I'm only eight!

TROY:
Ha, I see. So how come the coffee?

ROSA:
I've got a long day ahead of me!

TROY:
Oh, okay then! Well –

ROSA:
Bye, Felicia!

Rosa exits again with her hands holding two more "to go" cups.

Troy shakes his head, having been burned by a kid.

Friday comes. Troy sits with his newspaper, labelled Friday. His smart phone rings. The caller ID reads "SMOKEY'S".

Troy answers. As he's on the phone, he notices little Rosa coming in once again.

TROY: (on his phone)
Hello, yes, Mr. Robinson, yes, this is Troy. You still want me to come in on the first? No, oh... okay. Oh, come in next Friday instead. One week from today? You checked out my references and resume already? Great. I look forward to it.

Troy hangs up.

> **TROY**: (to himself)
> Man, this is visual manifestation stuff works!

Troy stands up from his chair in excitement.

Just then, little Rosa passes by him with her usual two coffees. Rosa and Troy collide by accident and the coffees hit the floor.

> **ROSA:**
> Oh no!

> **TROY**:
> Oh, my bad. Are you okay?

> **ROSA:** (almost hysterical)
> My mom's coffee and mine!

> **TROY**:
> Woah, it'll be all right, I'll take care of it.

> **ROSA:**
> But we're in a hurry, my mom has class.

> **TROY**:
> Okay, hold on. Here, you get some replacement coffees and I'll figure out this mess.

Troy opens his wallet and sees that he only has a five dollar bill in there. He hands it to Rosa and then looks around the coffee house.

Troy finds a closet and opens it up. He finds a mop and bucket.

Meanwhile, Rosa is back in line at the counter, waiting to get new coffees.

Troy comes back and cleans up the mess of spilled coffees and empty cups on the floor.

The coffee house door opens and Aaliyah comes in. She calls out to Rosa.

> **AALIYAH:**
> What's taking so long?
>
> **ROSA:**
> Mom, we had an accident. The man hit me.
>
> **AALIYAH:**
> Who hit my child?!

Rosa points out to Troy, cleaning up the mess, with the mop and bucket in his hand.

Aaliyah comes over to Troy.

> **AALIYAH:**
> Excuse me, did you touch my child?
>
> **TROY:**
> Uh, no, of course not --
>
> **AALIYAH:**
> Well, you better not have!

Rosa comes rushing over.

> **ROSA:**
> No, mommy it was an accident. Then he gave me money!

AALIYAH: (angry, to Troy)
You're giving money to my child, now? I've been sending her in here all week to avoid you myself and now you're trying to bribe my child!?

TROY:
No, uh, no, that's not what happened at all...

ROSA:
It's okay, mommy he's my friend. He's the 'modern man'.

Troy lifts up his book "The Modern Man's Guide to Self-Improvement" and gives Aaliyah an over-the-top smile.

Despite herself, Aaliyah enjoys this and her temperament calms down.

AALIYAH:
Well, now you've made me late for my class.

TROY:
Well, uh, you can still get in there, tell the teacher that you just had –

AALIYAH:
I am the teacher.

INT. EXERCISE ROOM - DAY

Troy, still in his street clothes, sweats up a storm as instructor Aaliyah leads a high energy "Zumba" type exercise class for about six other students.
Aaliyah barks out instructions as Troy struggles to keep up.

Little Rosa sits in the corner, with a doll in her hand, laughing at Troy.

Troy keeps his smile the whole time, although clearly uncomfortable and out of his element.

INT. ICE CREAM SPOT - DAY

NOTE: Coffee house location can double for this venue if necessary.

Troy, still perspiring from the class, wipes himself down with a bunch of paper napkins. Aaliyah looks him over.

> **AALIYAH:**
> You okay?
>
> **TROY**:
> Sure, never better.
>
> **AALIYAH:**
> You're a good sport, I'll give you that.
> **TROY**:
> Never surrender.
>
> **AALIYAH:**
> Okay, Rambo.
>
> **TROY**:
> How long you been into that stuff?
>
> **AALIYAH:**
> I'm not just 'into it'. It's my job. And I'm good at it.

Aaliyah lifts up a stack of Troy's used, damp napkins as evidence.

> **TROY**:
> Got me there.

Rosa comes to the table holding three cups of ice cream.

ROSA:
Here you go, mom. Here you go, Mister **Troy**.

AALIYAH:
Thank you, Rosa.

TROY:
Hey, I appreciate that... uh, let me pay for it...

Troy makes a half-hearted move for his wallet in his pants.

AALIYAH:
We already got you. You were a good sport today. Rosa, go wash your hands. The girls room is up front.

ROSA:
Yes, mom.

Rosa exits towards the bathrooms, leaving Aaliyah and troy alone again.

AALIYAH:
Let's call it even, okay?

TROY:
Even?

AALIYAH:
I was a bit harsh in the park.

TROY: (with a smile)
Harsh? More like rude. I ain't Jeffrey Dahmer.

AALIYAH:
Well, look, I'm a single mom and I can't take any

chances. Something happens to me, what's gonna happen to my little girl?

TROY:
Point taken.

AALIYAH:
And look, Troy, you're a nice guy and all. But at this stage of the game, please know, we can only be friends.

TROY: gives her an inquisitive look.

AALIYAH: (Cont'd)
I'm serious. Please, don't go there.

TROY:
Well, lucky for you, you're not my type.

AALIYAH:
I'm not, am I?

TROY:
Well, you know. Alpha woman. Bossy. Aggressive.

AALIYAH:
Oh... I see...

TROY:
Yeah... it just wouldn't work out, no physical attraction. I need a lady who I can get into.

AALIYAH:
Hmmm. I see.

Aaliyah points out the store window, where Monica, an African American woman, about 30, is entering the parking lot on foot.

AALIYAH: (Cont'd)
What about her? You think you could get into her?

Troy turns around and eyes her over.

TROY:
You know, I bet I could.

AALIYAH:
Why don't you give it a shot?

TROY:
What's on the line?

AALIYAH:
You get a date with her, I'll pay for it.

TROY:
Really?

AALIYAH:
Yeah.

Monica enters the ice cream shop. Troy approaches her.

TROY:
Uh, hello.

Monica:
Hello? You work here?

TROY:
Uh, welcome to World of Ice Cream.

Monica rolls her eyes a bit. Monica sees Aaliyah in the background, laughing to herself.

MONICA:
What you sellin'?

TROY:
Uh, we've got all types of great Ice Cream here. What can I interest you in?

MONICA:
Mmm... Rocky Road.

TROY:
You know what? We don't have Rocky Road today. Let me get your number and I'll call you when it comes in.

MONICA:
Oh, really, now?

TROY:
Yeah, as a matter of fact, let me make it up to you. I'll take you out for ice cream to another place, my treat.

MONICA:
You don't have to do that.

TROY:
No, no, I insist.

MONICA:
Okay, well. There is this new steakhouse I've been meaning to go to.

TROY:
Of course, a steakhouse...

MONICA:
And I heard they have the best sushi. And caviar. And cocktails!

TROY:
(tentative)
Oh yes, sounds great. Well, uh, it's a date.

Aaliyah is cracking up at her table.

MONICA:
Oh, just one thing...

TROY:
One thing...?

MONICA:
One condition. Can my sister come? To the restaurant? She's very pretty. And very outgoing.

TROY:
Uh, sure. Wow.

MONICA:
And my niece? Can my niece come too?

TROY:
Uh, how old's your niece?

Rosa comes out of the restroom just then and darts up to Monica.

ROSA:
Aunty!

MONICA:
Rosa, how old are you?

Monica and Aaliyah break into laughs, Troy finally catches on that he's been messed with.

> **TROY**:
> Oh, you got me. Y'all got me!

Aaliyah joins the fray.

> **AALIYAH:**
> Troy, this is my sister Monica. My older sister Monica.

> **MONICA:**
> Not that much older. But much more responsible.

> **TROY**:
> Oh, I see.

> **MONICA:**
> That's why Aunty Monica's here to pick up my favorite niece, 'cause someone promised to be the guest chaperone for her ballet class.
> Only thing is, my whip is overdue for an oil change and I was hoping -

Aaliyah pulls out her keys.

> **AALIYAH:**
> Take my Montero. Again.

> **MONICA:**
> (playing along in their familiar routine)
> Oh, really?

> **AALIYAH:**
> Of course.

ROSA:

We'll see you later, mommy. And you too, Mr. Troy!

TROY:

All right, then.

MONICA:

Don't forget the tournament starts next week, girl. We need you there! Nice meeting you, Troy.

Monica and Rosa exit.

TROY:

Hmmm. Wait, so, if she's got your car --?

AALIYAH:

I guess you're giving me a ride home. But first --

EXT. BEACH - DAY

Waves crash from the nearby ocean. Aaliyah and Troy walk onto the sand for the first time together, both having changed into beach attire.

AALIYAH:

The beach! I love it here!

She finds a set of rocks to sit on. Troy joins her.

Aaliyah looks out the water, a smile crosses her face. Troy gets caught up in looking at her.

TROY:

I can see why. It's beautiful. Hey, what did your sister mean by 'the tournament'? You in a bowling league or somethin'?

AALIYAH:
Poetry jam. You ever been to one?
TROY:
Poetry jam? Only jam I know goes on a biscuit.

AALIYAH:
Nah, it's fun. A bunch of us poets, we get together every week and there's a whole scene there. Once a year, there's a tournament.

TROY:
Y'all are nerds.

AALIYAH:
No, it's dope. My sister Monica runs the spot now. She took it over from...
(her words drift off and she changes the point of her sentence)
And I...I compete. Sometimes. That's where I met...

Her voice drifts off again. He leans in to see if she's going to finish her sentence but instead, she switches the attention back to Troy.

AALIYAH: (Cont'd)
You ain't never been to one?

TROY:
Nah.
AALIYAH:
You'd like it. I'll get you the info. You can come. Bring somebody.

TROY:
Who am I supposed to bring?

AALIYAH:
You'll find someone.

TROY:
I'll try. But I've been alone for so long, I'm getting used to that.

AALIYAH:
I haven't really been alone in years. I've got my daughter and my sister and my class and... This is my place to be alone. Nothing here but my clouds and my sun and my waves.

TROY:
What about me?

AALIYAH:
What about you?

Aaliyah stands up from the rocks, runs to the ocean, kicking her sandals off along the way.

She starts splashing around in the waves.

Troy stands on the beach for a moment, eying her over, before chasing her in.

They splash each other in fun and abandon.

A big wave comes and soaks Aaliyah, pulling her under the water.

Instinctively, Troy goes to her and scoops her up out of the water. A mouthful of ocean water comes out of her mouth.

After a couple of deep breaths, she regains her breathing, and turns to go back to the sand.

Troy grabs her by the arm to see if she's okay, she turns back to him, they lock eyes and kiss.

INT. VFW HALL BASEMENT - NIGHT

Troy sits in a circle with TWO OTHER MEN, ERIC, 40 and CRAIG, 27, and ONE WOMAN, CAROLINE, 55. A blackboard reads "Veterans Support Group."

There is one empty chair in the circle.

The Group Leader PAT, 45, (open gender), speaks first.

> **PAT:**
> Eric, Craig,... I'd like to introduce a new member to our little group, here. I believe Troy was brought to us by our own VIP member Caroline.

> **CAROLINE:**
> That's right, Pat.

> **PAT:**
> Troy, thank you for joining us.

> **TROY**:
> Thanks for having me.

> **CAROLINE:**
> (taking over the conversation before Pat can get started)
> This is your first time in a Vets group, right, Troy?

> **TROY**:
> Uh, yeah. I mostly... stick to myself.

CAROLINE:
Any thoughts as to why?

TROY:
Uh, just, I don't know. I guess I'm not good with... sharing. But I'm trying. To get better about it.

PAT:
Let's all please remember that we have a strict policy that nobody is forced to say any more here than they want to. This is a no pressure zone, agreed, everyone?

ERIC AND CRAIG: (TOGETHER)
Agreed.

CAROLINE:
(reluctant) Agreed.

TROY: (after an awkward silence, finally falling into line)
Yes, agreed.

PAT:
Troy, do you have any questions for us before we begin?
TROY:
Is there someone else coming?

The group all looks to the empty chair.

PAT:
Anyone?

ERIC
The empty chair represents the Missing Soldier --

PAT:
Or the Unknown Solider --

CAROLINE:
If you prefer. The Prisoner of War, the Missing in Action. Our brother - or sister - who didn't make it home and may never will.

Pat points to the POW/MIA flag on the wall.

PAT:
Until they're all home --

CRAIG:
None of us are home.

ERIC:
None of us are.

CRAIG:
None of us.

TROY:
I gotcha. Understood.
PAT: (checking his watch)
Okay, we've had our fun. Now, the meeting officially begins. Rules enforced. Phones off.

Everyone takes a moment to turn off their phones and put them away.

PAT: (Cont'd)
Eric, last time we left with you. You were telling us about your trouble sleeping.

ERIC:
Yeah, you know, I get these urges at night. --

CRAIG:
Urges? You mean like flashbacks?

The group leader PAT interrupts Craig interrupting Eric.

PAT:
Craig, remember rule number six. No cross talk.

CRAIG:
That's right. Sorry, Eric.

PAT:
Craig! No crosstalk!

CRAIG:
I was just apologizing!

TROY:
Hey, let's let Eric finish his story.

PAT:
Yes, good idea, Troy.

CAROLINE:
You're getting the hang of things, Troy.

ERIC:
Well, it's like these urges. Or flashbacks. Or whatever you want to call them. Just like...these violent images cross through my mind.

PAT:
About the war, Eric? Your time in the Middle East?

ERIC:
No, not really. More like my time here. Now. I get these really violent images across my mind and I

really have to work hard to keep myself in check. If I don't, I don't know what'll happen. What I'll do.
Something stupid.
Something sick.

The group reflects on this.

CAROLINE:
Eric, it's good for you to tell us about these issues. But - if you're really feeling this way - like you're getting out of control, you've got to tell your wife. You've got to get back to your doctor and ask for those medications –

PAT:
Uhm, hold on there, Caroline, you know that we aren't allowed to offer other members advice like that. We're here for support. No judgement. And no recommendations.

CAROLINE:
But I –

PAT:
Caroline, please. We all know the rules. We're a support group. No judgement. And no advice.

CAROLINE:
This isn't about advice, Pat, this is about people's lives! Their safety!

PAT:
That's enough, Caroline. Now, if you want to speak on your own week, go right ahead. Perhaps you can cheer us up a bit.

CAROLINE:
Well, my ex-husband is getting out of jail next Tuesday and he's telling people already that he's gonna find me and kill me. How's that for a cheer me up?

PAT:
Ugh. Craig, how about you?

CRAIG:
Well, you know, just the same. Still unemployed and sleeping on my mother's couch with the dog.

PAT:
Troy, do you have anything to share?

All eyes turn to Troy...

TROY:
Uh...I was at the beach with a chick this morning and we ended up making out in the ocean.

Caroline chuckles and the guys look on in awe at Troy's reveal.

CAROLINE:
Wow, sure sounds like you had a better day than all of us.

PAT:
Do you think there is potential for this relationship long-term?

TROY:
Ummm...I would think so, uhh uhh but...

CAROLINE:
What's the baggage, champ?

TROY:
Baggage...what do you mean?

CAROLINE:
If it really worked so great this morning between you two, you wouldn't be sitting here with all of us.

Caroline extends her hands out to indicate the whole group of lost souls.

ERIC:
Yeah buddy, if you're gonna try to escape our island of misfit toys, it better be with the right girl.

TROY:
Well, here's the thing... the lady's great but she's got a little girl. The kid is awesome and a real sweetheart. And I could see it all working out for us as a family...

Troy's voice drifts off as the other members of the group become more attuned to what he's saying.

TROY: (Cont'd)
It's just that I never thought I would ever be in a relationship with a woman that has a kid.
Already. That isn't mine.

Group members all look to each other and then back to Troy.

CAROLINE:
Troy, I've been around the block --

PAT:
Caroline, remember that --

CAROLINE: (with authority)
I'm gonna say what I'm gonna say, Pat.

Pat recoils in his chair.

CAROLINE: (Cont'd)
You know I've been around the block and I have had a few battles with love and war kid. I've been against the ropes of loneliness and isolation, but I've come out swinging against those adversaries. I realize something worth having is worth fighting for. If this woman is worth it to you. Troy, then fight for her! Don't let her slip past you. As far as her little girl goes, don't let the fact that your seed didn't plant that pumpkin take the orange off the shell.

Troy rubs his chin to contemplate on her words.

EXT. DOWNTOWN SIDEWALK - NIGHT

Troy walks the city sidewalk past local businesses en route to the poetry club.

EXT. CLUB EXPRESSIONS - NIGHT

Troy sees the marquee of Club Expressions. Troy sees group of HIPSTERS, POETS, and assorted WEIRDOS.

Troy, feeling a bit out of place already, walks by everyone and into the club.

INT. CLUB EXPRESSIONS - NIGHT

We follow Troy as he makes his way through the crowd for her but his eyes become filled with the sight of ASSORTED BOHEMIANS and even MORE POETS.

> **TROY**: (to himself)
> One day at a time.

Troy approaches the bar.

He sees an EMO BARTENDER. She's got multiple tattoos and body piercings with dark black hair.

She comes over to Troy with a bit of an attitude.

> **EMO BARTENDER:** (not nice at all)
> What do you want, man?

> **TROY**:
> Uh, you got anything non-alcoholic?

Emo Bartender laughs in Troy's face.

> **EMO BARTENDER:**
> This is a Kombucha bar, sir...

> **TROY**:
> Is kombuchee alcoholic?

> **EMO BARTENDER:** (lightening up a little bit)
> No, it's not. It's good for you. Probiotics.

She points to the sign that lists 19 flavors of Kombucha

> **TROY**: (puzzled)
> Pro-bi-who?

> **EMO BARTENDER:** (slowly, as if talking to an idiot)
> What *flavor* of Kombucha, sir? We have nineteen flavors to choose from.

Troy shakes his head in confusion and leaves the bar area. He sees Aaliyah at a table by herself, right in the center of the club.

She soaks in the candlelight at the table, the flames flickering against her cheekbones and dancing in her eyes.

Troy pushes his way through the crowd of POETS and HIPSTERS en route to her table.
Aaliyah looks up to see him.

> **AALIYAH:**
> Hey, you made it.

She stands and gives him a warm but non passionate hug.

He moves in for a kiss on her lips, but she twists her neck to leave his lips only to land on her cheek.

> **TROY**:
> Oh, I see...

She ignores his statement.

> **AALIYAH:**
> Hey, you look good at night. Next time, though, don't be such a stiff.

Troy looks down to his pants, fearing that something 'came up' during their hug.

TROY:
What?

AALIYAH:
Your outfit. It's a little... boring. This place has got a certain, you know, vibe.

She extends her hand to "present" the crowd of hipsters to him.

TROY:
Okay. Well, I'm a little too old to die my hair pink or pierce my eyeballs. But maybe a tattoo of Spongebob? How do you think that would fly?

AALIYAH:
Now, now, don't get hostile. Where's your drink?

TROY:
The menu was in a foreign language, 'Hipster Pretentiousness'.

AALIYAH:
It's kombucha. You don't like it?

TROY: (whispering, as if admitting a dark secret)
I've got to admit something. Very personal.

AALIYAH:
What's up?

TROY:
I've never had 'kombuchee'.

AALIYAH:
You got to know how to order. Allow me.

Troy watches her as she leaves to go back to the bar he was just at. Her toned body glistens in her dress as she leans over to talk with the bartender. Aaliyah and the bartender interact like old friends.

Although the venue has a fairly filled CROWD, Troy's attention is solely on Aaliyah. A glow from lights on the bar heighten her importance in his focus, creating an angelic glow around her.

Aaliyah looks over from the bar to see Troy eyeing her over.
She returns to him with two fresh bottles of Kombucha, one in each hand.

As she walks back to him, from Troy's POV, it's like an angel is coming to him from Heaven itself.

> **AALIYAH:** (Cont'd)
> See something you like?
>
> **TROY:**
> I most certainly do.
>
> **AALIYAH:**
> What's your flavor?
>
> **TROY:** (flirting)
> Mocha chocolate.
>
> **AALIYAH:**
> Uh, no. The Kombucha. I got Apple Pear Sunrise and Cranberry Crescent Moon. One for you and one for me. Since you're my guest, I'll let you pick.
>
> **TROY:**
> Ah, damn. How can I decide, they're both so tempting?

AALIYAH:
Take the Apple Pear. It will be good for you.

TROY:
Yes, ma'am.

AALIYAH:
Now, pull out my chair. We're just friends but I'm still a lady.

TROY:
All right, then.

Troy pulls out her chair for her.

She sits in it. He continues to admire her, then takes the seat next to her. As she sips from the Cranberry Kombucha bottle, he continues to admire her, as her face glows in the candlelight.

AALIYAH:
Boy, you better stop --

TROY:
I gotta ask you somethin'.

AALIYAH:
What's up?

TROY:
This 'just friends' stuff... Who you tryin' to kid? Me or you?

AALIYAH:
Mmm. Tough question, TROY:. You're a good man. But... it's complicated.

TROY:
You got a kid, I got that. But I think I can handle it.

AALIYAH:
You 'think' you can?

TROY:
I've got my own problems, too.

AALIYAH:
My daughter is not a problem.

TROY:
I didn't mean it like that. I mean... you know, it's not easy.

AALIYAH:
Nothing's easy, champ. Just friends. There are plenty of girls in this place I can introduce you to.

Troy looks around the bar. The assorted POETRY PRINCESSES are unique and funky, but none catch his eye like Aaliyah does herself.

TROY:
You know, none of these girls were kissing me in the ocean recently. Where were those girls then?

Aaliyah looks to him, not sure how to retort. They share a tense moment of trying to read each other.

Before either can speak, Club Expression's overhead lights do a "slow flicker" then fade down until the whole club is dark.
    TROY: (Cont'd)
    What's going on? Fire drill?

A guttural scream comes from the front of the club.

Then a singular word, with a raw urgency, is repeated into a microphone, in the darkness.

> **MONICA:** (O.S.) (in mic)
> House. House. HOUSE.

A spotlight comes onto a singular bar stool on stage with a "Raggedy Annie" type doll sitting on top of it.

> **TROY**: (at their table in a hushed voice)
> What the...?

> **AALIYAH:**
> Shhh. This is great.

Another spotlight appears on stage onto Monica, Aaliyah's sister. She is dressed up in her poetry goddess best outfit.

> **AALIYAH:** (at their table)
> You go, girl.

On stage, Monica screams again to get EVERYONE'S attention. Many in the AUDIENCE begin to snap their fingers and nod their head in a ritualistic manner as if they've done this many times before.

> **TROY**: (at their table)
> That's your sister, right? Is she okay? Should I call somebody?

> **AALIYAH:** (at their table)
> Shhhh. She's fine. It's performance art.

On stage, Monica stops screaming and breaks into a "Spoken Word Poet" performance voice.

MONICA: (Cont'd...in mic)
House, are you with me tonight?

Some reaction of affirmations from the crowd.

MONICA: (Cont'd...in mic)
I said, House, are you WITH me TONIGHT?

Now, the crowd really gets into it.

MONICA: (Cont'd...in mic)
That's what I'm talking about. The Fresh Prince said it. Sometimes parents of the World just don't understand.

The CROWD breaks into some knowing "Uh Huhs" and other vocal affirmations.

MONICA: (Cont'd...in mic)
Too often, us older folk forget what's it like to be a kid. We look at the younger generation and feel they are not living up to our certain expectations. Nothing is ever good enough to give us our craving for satisfaction... to have our kids be like us.

The spotlight goes back on the Raggedy Ann type doll on the barstool.

MONICA: (Cont'd...in mic)
None of us consented to be here in the first place...so why do we need parental consent to live the way we intend to for the rest of our lives? Tonight, if no one else, will, I, Mistress Monica, give you permission. Tonight, enjoy yourselves. No judgement. Be a kid.

The CROWD applauds, calls out more affirmations and snaps.

> **MONICA**: (Cont'd...in mic)
> Remember, House, that next week is the Wild Card round of our annual Heartbreak Poetry Tournament. Yes, our returning three-time champion Brett Harris is scheduled to take a break from his worldwide spoken word tour to return to us here at Club Expressions to defend his title.

The crowd erupts into applause and excitement hearing the name "Brett Harris".

At their table, Aaliyah's face reveals a bit of discomfort.

> **TROY**:
> You okay?
>
> **AALIYAH:**
> I'm good. Must be the Kombucha.

Troy looks at his bottle suspiciously.

> **MONICA**: (in mic)
> Now, wait, a minute, y'all. The defending champ doesn't have to qualify but he does still have to win.

A Random Cynical Voice comes from the crowd.

> **RANDOM CYNICAL VOICE # 1:**
> Brett can't be beat!

The crowd oohs and ahhs at the Random Voice's declaration.

> **MONICA**: (Cont'd...in mic)
> Now, wait a minute, y'all. Brett Harris can be beat. Just some of you mother-truckers need to step up your game. Like Oliver Stone said, Any Given

> Sunday. Or Saturday. Or Wednesday night. Maybe it's time we have a new King - or Queen - of the poetry scene. But to be the man, you gotta beat the man. And Brett Harris will be here to defend his title. You can count on it.

The crowd oohs and ahhs again. At their table, Troy continues to look around is discomfort.

> **MONICA**: (Cont'd…in mic)
> But we'll let that tournament take care of itself. Tonight, it's a Free Style Open Heart, Open Mind, Open Mic Night you dig. And we got a Heckler J, waiting to take you fools to another level. You dig?

The crowd responds.

> **MONICA**: (Cont'd…in mic)
> I said…
> (in her best "Cyrus" from "Warriors" voice)
> Can... you... dig... it?

HECKLER J, a short poet with a MIME/CLOWN/JUGGLER "character" type persona, waddles out onto the stage.

The crowd erupts in laughter.

> **TROY**: (to Monica, at their table)
> What is up with this shiznet?

Aaliyah just hushes him with a finger to his lips to indicate him to shut up.
Back on stage, Heckler J does a little juggling routine, getting a big crowd response. Then, he breaks into his poetry.

> **HECKLER J**: (in mic)
> What we see triggers a thought... this begins a pattern and starts like a washing machine. We absorb thoughts like a sponge and it feeds us a hearty meal of words! What we speak from our tongues is either life or death. However, it's what we keep under our own breath that is like lava waiting to erupt. Don't mean to be so abrupt, just seeing what's corrupt?

At their table, Troy is terribly uncomfortable and shocked that everyone else is enjoying themselves.

> **TROY**: (at their table)
> Yo, Aaliyah, is this a cult? Did you bring me into some scientology shit? Where's the King of Queens lady to save my ass?

Suddenly, the crowd goes fully quiet. Heckler J stops his performance immediately.

With all eyes piercing him, Troy finally realizes he spoke too loud and his words were heard by everyone in the club.

Another spotlight finds its way over to Troy and Aaliyah's table and lands on Troy.

> **TROY**: (Cont'd...under his breath)
> Oh, shit. They gonna kill me? This some Eyes Wide Shut shit?

Aaliyah melts from embarrassment in her chair.
A few members of the Crowd break into nervous laughter at Troy's words.

Back on stage, Heckler J, addresses the situation and Troy directly, who is still under the bright spotlight at his table with Aaliyah in the center of the club.

> **HECKLER J:** (speaking loudly without use of the microphone)
> First time at Club Expressions, sir?

At his table, Troy has no choice but to interact.

> **TROY**:
> Yes, I'm afraid so.

> **HECKLER J:** (back into the mic)
> Afraid? There's nothing here to fear, sir.

Heckler J takes a dramatic moment and goes into a Shakespearean verse.

> **HECKLER J:** (Cont'd)
> 'If we shadows have offended, think but this and all is mended, that you have but slumbered here, While these visions did appear. And this weak and idle theme, No more yielding but a dream, Gentles, do not reprehend: If you pardon, we will mend.'

The Crowd applauds.

> **HECKLER J:** (Cont'd…in mic, to Troy:)
> In case you didn't recognize, that was a bit of Shakespeare, sir.

The Crowd oohs and ahhs, expecting conflict between Heckler J and Troy.

Troy looks over the Crowd. He studies everyone's faces, staring at him, wondering how he will respond. He feels their judgement, their curiosity, their fear. Troy rises to his feet.

> **TROY**: (loudly, addressing the whole Club with a surprising confidence and likability)
> It was indeed Puck from Shakespeare's A Midsummers Night Dream. Act Five, Scene One. One of my favorites. And you performed it quite well, as a man with a steady word of seemingly great authenticity and compassion. And now, allow me to apologize, not only to you, kind sir, but to all my fellow patrons in this wonderful establishment.
>
> You see, I have served. I have served in the United States military. Air Force. Security Forces Raven. And we fought. We fought for our freedoms. And we fought for the freedoms of others. The freedom to love. The freedom to hate. The freedom to speak. And perhaps, when I came in here tonight, I had somehow forgotten, what true speech is.
>
> What true expression is. Expression is not to be judged; it is help all to evolve. So, please forgive me, all. Tonight was my fist taste of...

Troy lifts us his bottle from the table.

> **TROY**: (Cont'd)
> Kombucha. Peach Apple Sunrise. It's a little different at first, I must admit, but I'm beginning to enjoy the taste. So, please, all, accept my humble apologies for my rudeness and allow me to raise a toast to you, kind sir. To your boldness. To your compassion. To your performance. And please... speak on.

Troy raises a toast with his bottle of Kombucha to everyone in the club.

Just about everyone goes along with it. Aaliyah looks up to Troy with a shocked face, with a tinge of admiration.

Monica walks by their table and she and her sister Aaliyah silently communicate their shock with their eyes and subtle raised eyebrows to each other.

On stage, Heckler J nods in a surprised but pleased approval of Troy's action and the corresponding Crowd's reaction.

> **HECKLER J:** (in mic)
> All right then, kind sir. Welcome to 'Club Expressions'. Enjoy your evening, sir. And thank you for your service. And please... join us, anytime.

Troy smiles and raises a tip of his bottle to Heckler J. The CROWD applauds in the show of mutual respect.

A WAITRESS brings Troy and Aaliyah's table a complimentary platter of hummus and pita chips, that they snack on as they watch the evening's entertainment unfold.

Various POETS take the stage, all delivering verse in their own unique voices.

BOB, 60, who has a bad leg and uses crutches, gets up on stage with some help from Monica.

Bob has a curmudgeonly look and affect to his presence. Bob takes the mic.

> **BOB:** (in mic)
> People hold grudges like they got a wedgie stuck up their ass! Don't let grudges be like a kidney

stone. It will pass but is sure will hurt like hell.

At their table, Troy and Aaliyah share a smile.

> **BOB**: (Cont'd…in mic)
> Life is too short to be holding grudges. You block your blessings like a blocked artery. Grudges are like blood-clots. Like the old saying goes, a hard head makes a soft ass.

At their table, Troy shakes his head in appreciation.

> **BOB**: (Cont'd…in mic)
> When we know better, we tend to do much better. Bury those grudges like a dog burying a bone.

This lesson resonates with Troy.

Back on stage, the next poet DEBORAH, 40, a regular poet, kind of a frumpy librarian vibe, takes the stage.

> **DEBORAH:** (in mic)
> Here's the thing, some people that are together are not even in a relationship. They are a thing with nothing that defines their relationship status. Friends with benefits, with no strings attached may be the model but neither one of them has exactly hit the lottery of love.

Meanwhile, Troy continues to look over to Aaliyah, captivated by her beauty.

Monica comes over to their table.

> **MONICA:**
> Hey, you two, having fun?

AALIYAH:
Most definitely, girl.

MONICA:
Hey, sis, you-know-who will be back here in two weeks.

AALIYAH:
Umm...hmmm.
TROY: (curious)
Who's 'you know who'?

MONICA:
Brett Harris, the --

AALIYAH:
Defending champion. He's won the poetry tournament two years in a row.

TROY:
Um. Good for him.

AALIYAH:
Yeah, he's all right.

TROY:
Maybe he just needs some real competition.

AALIYAH:
Yeah. Maybe.

MONICA: (to Troy)
And you? You made quite the impression on everyone tonight.

TROY:
Really?

MONICA:
Really. That kombucha toast? My word. So, you gonna give next week a shot?

TROY:
What do you mean?

AALIYAH: (not liking where this is headed)
Yeah... what do you mean?

MONICA:
Wildcard night in the big tournament. Voice of Jacksonville. We've got two open spots. And one has got your name on it.

AALIYAH:
I don't know if that's a good idea, Monica --

TROY:
Who's name? Mine?

MONICA:
That's right, Troy. You. Up for the challenge, stud? We could use another Alpha Male around here to step up and challenge Brett Harris.

AALIYAH: (under her breath)
Girl, don't go there.

TROY: (not hearing Aaliyah, responding only to Monica)
I guess so... I don't like to back down... from anything.

MONICA:
All right, then. We might have ourselves a little rooster fight in the henhouse.

Monica goes over to the bar quickly to grab something from Emo Bartender.

At their table, Troy looks to Aaliyah.

TROY:
Your sister's a trip.

AALIYAH:
Yeah. Like bad acid.

TROY:
So, I guess... I'm a poet?

AALIYAH: (awkward)
I... guess so... you sure you want to do this?

Troy looks up to the stage as a GOOFY POET recites a really bad poem.

GOOFY POET: (into mic)
I am the Toaster Oven of love! I reheat the left-overs of love, the pop-tarts of love, the frozen pizzas of love! I am the Toaster Oven of love!

At the table, Troy shakes his head in confidence.

TROY: (to Aaliyah, mocking Goofy Poet)
If he can do it, I can do it. For,
I am... the microwave oven of love!

Back on stage, Goofy Poet continues.

> **GOOFY POET:** (into mic)
> I collect the burnt crumbs of your love and let them
> burn to a smoke!

Back at their table, Monica returns with a clipboard and a sign-up sheet.

It reads "WILDCARD POETS". There are six signatures on it already with the number 7 and a blank line.

Monica puts the clipboard in front of Troy.

> **MONICA:**
> There you go.
>
> **TROY**:
> Lucky number seven!

Troy looks to Aaliyah. She has a tense look on her face, that he does not recognize for what it is.

Troy signs his signature.

Monica lifts up her clipboard and reads his name aloud.

> **MONICA:**
> Lucky number seven is…Troy Wilson!

Troy fist pumps at the table.
> **TROY**:
> All right!

Aaliyah shakes her head at Monica in a "no, you didn't" fashion.

> **MONICA:**
> It should be fun, Troy!

Troy smiles. Aaliyah gives her sister a hard look. Monica returns it with a sarcastic smile and a roll of her eyes.

Troy smiles again, not catching their interaction.

Aaliyah bites into a pita chip with ferocity and it snaps violently.

INT. TROY'S CAR - NIGHT

Troy drives with a big smile on his face and talks about the upcoming poetry tournament he is suddenly a part of.

> **TROY**:
> I can't believe it! My first week at the poetry jam and next week I'm in the tournament! I gotta write some stuff. I gotta get some threads. You gotta help me!

Aaliyah sits in shotgun, distracted but trying to pay attention to him.

> **AALIYAH:** (placating to him)
> Mmmm, hmmm.

Meanwhile, she texts her sister Monica frantically.

Text on Aaliyah's phone: "What is up w you???!! Are you serious?! Bretts gonna be there!"

Response Text back from Monica: "I thought TROY was just a friend. (Curious face emoji with the 'shrug hands'.)"

Aaliyah's text back: MYOBB

Aaliyah angrily chucks her phone into her purse.

TROY:
Man, I'm gonna kill next week!

AALIYAH:
It's a poetry tournament not a demolition derby, Troy.

EXT. AALIYAH'S HOME - NIGHT

Troy parks his car outside Aaliyah's townhouse.

INT. TROY'S CAR - NIGHT

Troy, still with a wide smile, and Aaliyah, still tense, pull up in front of her townhouse.

TROY:
So, who all's in there?
AALIYAH:
Huh?

TROY:
Who do you, uh, live with?

AALIYAH:
My sister. Who've you met. And my daughter. Who you've met.

TROY:
I see. And... that's it?

AALIYAH: (changing the subject)
Thanks for the ride, Troy. You really don't have to do the poetry thing. If you don't want to.

TROY:
Oh, I want to.

AALIYAH:
Well, you know, I'm probably gonna compete in the tournament too. And I, I wouldn't want it to be... awkward.

TROY:
Not awkward for me. Awkward for you?

AALIYAH:
Well, no. I just... you know, don't want you to feel bad once I beat you.

TROY:
Oh, okay.

AALIYAH:
There'd be nothing wrong for you to gracefully bow out at this point. Nobody's expecting much from you.

TROY:
I'm expecting much from me.

AALIYAH:
Seriously, Troy, it's all right for you to watch as a fan. You don't have to compete. This is really not your crowd.

TROY:
You kidding me? Those people loved my kombuchee speech. And besides, your sister invited me into the tournament.

AALIYAH:
That's true. She did. I'll have to talk with her about that.

TROY:
And besides, I put my name on the dotted line. My signature is as good as my word. And my word is good as gold.

AALIYAH:
Okay, then. And, for the record, I do respect you for being open minded. It's refreshing. Thank you for a wonderful evening. You might make for a good friend, Troy.

Aaliyah goes to open her door. But the door is locked. She turns to look at Troy, but his seat is now empty.

She looks back to her side and Troy has now opened her car door for her.

He extends his hand to help her out of her seat.

AALIYAH: (Cont'd)
All right, then.

EXT. AALIYAH:'S HOME - NIGHT

Aaliyah and Troy stand outside. He has a wide-eyed look of romance in his eyes that is hard for her to ignore.

He continues to hold her hand in his.

TROY:
Aaliyah. Aaliyah. Your name is like poetry. Aaliyah. I can't help but magnify the beautiful creation that stands before me.

You're impossible to ignore me. You're like a door that leads me to my destiny. I just have to find the key that mysteries of your love.

Aaliyah covers his lips with a singular index finger to silence him.

He grabs her finger gently and kisses it.

AALIYAH:
No, no, no. Troy, you gotta stop.

TROY:
What... what you mean?

AALIYAH:
'Just friends', I told you.
TROY:
What's going on here? Everything's so perfect. And then you put the brake's on...?

AALIYAH:
I've got a kid.

TROY:
I know that. Rosa. She's great. This ain't about her. It's about you. And me. What gives?
AALIYAH:
Rosa's got a dad.

TROY:
Well, most people do. I know how biology works.

AALIYAH:
Yeah, but... remember tonight, when... when Monica talked about the Poetry Champion? Brett Harris?

TROY:
Huh? I guess so. I heard it, what does that have to do with me? Some chump poet I gotta beat along my way?

AALIYAH:
He's no chump. It's him. It's Brett. It's Brett Harris. He's Rosa's dad. My 'sort of' ex.

TROY:
'Sort of'!? So, does he live here too with y'all?

AALIYAH:
Well, like, it's complicated.

TROY:
Complicated?! You with this guy or not?

AALIYAH:
Sort of. Sort of not. We're on a break but... there always hope of us working it out.

TROY:
'Hope'? You guys working it out or not?

AALIYAH:
I...don't know. Troy, when you gotta kid with somebody, it's complicated. I don't expect you to understand. I didn't want to lead you on but... you're a nice guy and...

TROY:
Oh, the 'nice guy' crap. I've heard that line from women my whole life.

Aaliyah just stands there, not sure how to respond.

TROY: (Cont'd)
So, what's with bringing me to this poetry jam on a date for? Just to show him up? You using me as a bargaining chip to play against him?

AALIYAH:
No, no. He wasn't even gonna be there tonight so I thought it would be nice to invite you. As a 'one-off' thing. I didn't really think you'd like it. And make such a spectacle of yourself.

TROY:
Well, I do like it. And I like you. And I'm not a 'sort of' on, 'sort of' off type of guy. With me? It's all or nothing. How 'bout that?

AALIYAH:
Your boldness is strong, honey, but that ain't the real world I'm livin' in. There are shades of grey to this shit.

TROY:
Give me a break. Seems to me you were putting out feelers for some side-dick.

Her face registers shock at his words, knocking her speechless for a second.

AALIYAH:
Oh, no, you didn't.

TROY:
Oh yes, I damn well did.

She is about to go off on him but then lowers her volume, trying to calm the situation if at all possible.

AALIYAH:
Don't overblow this thing. Like I said... I can introduce you to other girls. There are other women besides me, Troy. And I want you to like the poetry scene, Troy. If you have found a place to express yourself, don't let my drama get in your way. Brett's a good guy and maybe deep down I thought, just maybe, you and me and him... we could all be friends...

TROY:
You all freaks or what? I ain't into that shit.

AALIYAH:
It ain't like that. I haven't even seen him in weeks. He's been on tour.

TROY:
Tour? Is he in Van Halen? The Circus? What kind of mother fucker goes on tour when he's got a wife and kid at home?

AALIYAH:
We ain't never been married. And it's a poetry tour.

TROY:
A poetry tour?! What kind of crap is that?

AALIYAH:
He sells his books. Out of his car. And he performs in bookstores and coffee houses throughout the country. Right now, he's in Portland, then Seattle, then he'll be home in two weeks for the tournament.

TROY:
That pay y'all's bills?

AALIYAH:
Um, sometimes. It helps. But mostly we get by on my work at the gym.

TROY:
How many green-haired poetry skeezas you think ol' Brett is banging in Portland this week?

Stunned by his harshness, she mistakenly causes him the wrong name then corrects herself.

AALIYAH:
Brett! I mean, Troy, that ain't fair!

Troy looks her over, judging her with cruel eyes.

TROY:
'W is for Winner'. How's for that for a poem?

Troy goes back to his side of the car and opens the door.

Aaliyah cries out to him.

AALIYAH:
I didn't lie to you, Troy! I just didn't....

He gets in the car, slam his door shut, starts the engine in a huff, and drives off quick.

AALIYAH: (Cont'd...standing there, to herself)
...tell you the truth.

INT. TROY'S CAR - NIGHT

Troy drives, his face intense.

He puts on music. A modern day song - something like Tupac's 'Changes' - come on.

Troy's face reflects the same frustration of the song's lyrics.

EXT. JACKSONVILLE - NIGHT

Troy continues to drive, passing through several neighborhoods. The streets are mostly empty, and everything is at a standstill, to match Troy's mood.

Another song comes on which also matches Troy's mood.

EXT. BEACH - NIGHT

Troy walks out onto the beach himself, on the same path that he and Aaliyah once walked on together.

Troy has a bottle of alcohol in his hand.

Troy finds the same set of rocks that he and Aaliyah sat on together. Troy sits on the rocks.

He looks at the bottle of alcohol in his hand, reading the label carefully out loud, including the alcohol content level.

Troy pulls out a wooden token from his pocket. He reads it.

INSERT SHOT: COIN OF SOBRIETY - 1,000 days of sobriety. One day at a time.

Troy twists the coin in his fingers, looking at it over and over.

Troy takes the bottle of alcohol. He grips the cap, as if to twist it open. But he does not.

Then he raises the bottle over his head, as if to smash it against the rocks. But he does not.

Troy erupts into deep breathing, then heavy tears as if having a panic attack.

He slumps against the rocks.

Night falls over him.

EXT. BEACH - SUNRISE (THE NEXT MORNING)

Troy awakens, still in his clothes from the night before.

He is disheveled, a mess.

He reaches into his pocket.

He pulls out the same wooden token. The Coin of Sobriety.

Troy looks over to the ground near him.

He sees the bottle of alcohol, planted in the sand, half covered.

It was never opened.

Troy smiles.

He clenches his coin.

TROY: (to himself)
One day at a time.

INT. TROY'S BATHROOM - MORNING

Troy takes a shower, the water splashing onto his face, waking him up.

INT. TROY'S KITCHEN - MORNING

Troy sits at his lonely kitchen table. A box of Entenmann's Chocolate Doughnuts sit there. He bites into one.

He opens his refrigerator. He sees a jar of Orange Juice, he grabs it. Upon further inspection, Troy realizes the Juice is old and spoiled.

TROY: (to himself)
Damn.

Troy sees the toaster oven in his kitchen.

TROY: (Cont'd...to himself)
Toaster oven of love. Reheated crumbs and shit.

Troy laughs to himself.

He sits down again at the table.

He begins to look through the classifieds again.

Then he picks up his phone and makes a call, on speaker.

The phone answers.

MR. ROBINSON: (voice on speaker)
Hello?

TROY:
Hello, Mr. Robinson, sir?

MR. ROBINSON: (voice on speaker)
Yeah, that's my name. Don't wear it out, now.

TROY:
Okay, Mr. Robinson. It's Troy Wilson, I'm scheduled for an in-person interview to be your new cook in a few days.

MR. ROBINSON: (voice on speaker)
Mmm. Hmm. That's right. It ain't Friday now, already, is it son?

TROY:
No, sir. I just wanted to confirm in advance.

MR. ROBINSON: (voice on speaker)
Mmm. Very professional of you, Troy. I checked your credentials and I look forward to meeting you. Only thing that might be a hold up is this Carolina virus.

TROY:
Carolina virus?

MR. ROBINSON: (voice on speaker)
Check yo' newspaper. There's some virus from the Carolinas threatening to take over the world.

TROY:
You serious?

> **MR. ROBINSON:** (voice on speaker)
> Check yo' paper. If we ain't all dead by then, I'll see you Friday.

Click. Mr. Robinson hangs up.

Troy shakes his head, confused.

> **TROY:** (to himself)
> Carolina virus?

Troy looks through his newspaper until he finds the news section.

A headline reads "Coronavirus aka Covid-19 sweeps China; sanctions expected".

Troy begins to read the article.

> **TROY**: (Cont'd…to himself)
> What kinda shit is this?

INT. COFFEE HOUSE - DAY

Troy now sits at his usual table, sipping coffee and reading an article about Coronavirus.

Troy pulls out a Sports magazine. The cover story reads "Kobe Bryant and daughter die in helicopter crash".

> **TROY**: (to himself, under his breath)
> What a crazy year. Hope it turns around.

Troy looks up to see Rosa, Aaliyah's daughter, enter.

Rosa makes a bee-line to the counter to order, seemingly not looking in Troy's direction at all. Troy checks out the window and he has to crane his neck to see that Aaliyah is parked clear across the street.

Troy observes as Rosa orders two drinks to go.
Rosa gets the drinks and passes by Troy.

> **ROSA:**
> I'm not supposed to talk to you, if you're here.
>
> **TROY:**
> I understand. Your mom mad at me?
>
> **ROSA:**
> I think she's scared.
>
> **TROY:**
> Scared? Really?
>
> **ROSA:**
> She said you were really mad.

Rosa exits.

Troy looks down at his paper for a minute looking at the photo of Kobe and his daughter.

Troy gets up, determined, and exits the coffee house.

EXT. PARKING LOT - DAY

Troy goes across the lot and sees Rosa entering her mom's car on the passenger's side.

Troy approaches with caution. He catches up to Aaliyah just after she helps Rosa get into the car and before she gets into her car herself.

TROY:
Aaliyah.

AALIYAH:
Troy? We gotta go.

TROY:
Hey, hear me out.

AALIYAH:
I'm sorry, Troy, I can't give you what you need or be more to you.

TROY:
And I'm sorry that my emotions ran wild. I've got a problem with... intensity. I'd never hurt you... but you don't know that.

AALIYAH:
No, I don't. Why do you care so much, Troy?

TROY:
Before we met, I was but a horse dwelling in the stable. On the exterior, I exuded an assuring confidence and steady calmness, however, truthfully on the inside, I just wanted to run away to secure my freedom. Several times throughout my life, I've been reminded the grass isn't always greener on the other side. I've always been a lone star and I'm determined to find my way. I know we just met and I know you have other possible destinies. I'm just glad you slowed down enough for me to get your attention. I don't want to be a distraction, yet I desire to be your main attraction.

She looks him over. Then gives him a big smile.

AALIYAH:
A horse? More like a jackass.

TROY:
Hey...

AALIYAH:
Nobody's perfect, Troy. Not me, not you, not anybody.

TROY:
There is actually one perfect soul.

AALIYAH:
Well, whatever. I forgive you for getting upset and you can forgive me if I lead you on. That fair?

Troy smiles.

TROY:
Depends.

AALIYAH:
Oh?

TROY:
What's the status with 'on again, off again'?

AALIYAH:
Let's say it was on 'off'. What would it matter? I don't think your built to keep up with me, anyway.

TROY:
Is that a challenge?

AALIYAH:

And what if it is?

TROY:
What's on the line?

INT. GYM - DAY

They are both on exercise bikes, facing the same direction, Troy's already broken into a sweat, while Aaliyah is still dry and comfortable.

Rosa watches, amused, from a corner of the room.

> **AALIYAH:** (while cycling)
> You last the hour with me until 3pm, you get one date. One.

Troy looks up at the clock. It's one of those old industrial school building clocks. It's only 2:04pm.

> **TROY**: (while cycling)
> And what kind of date we talking about?

> **AALIYAH:** (while cycling)
> Surprise me. Your choice.

MONTAGE:

Aaliyah and Troy cycle against each other.
An epic rock song - like something from a Rocky movie - plays during their challenge.

> **AALIYAH:** (Cont'd…while cycling)
> C'mon now, keep up the pace.

> **TROY**: (while cycling)
> I'm keepin', I'm keepin'!

The overhead CLOCK on the wall taunts Troy as it moves ever so slow.

> **AALIYAH:** (while cycling)
> Lookin' at that clock ain't gonna move faster.
>
> **TROY**: (while cycling)
> No pain, no gain, baby.

F/X: Time Lapse photography: The clock advances to 55 minutes past the hour.

> **AALIYAH:** (while cycling)
> Wow, you just might make it. Big sprint to the finish!

Aaliyah increases her speed. Troy keeps up as best he can.

> **TROY**: (while cycling)
> I... won't... back... down.

Troy eyeballs the clock. It stays at 2:59 pm for a seeming eternity.

The clock ticks BACKWARDS a click, back to 2:58pm. Troy stops cycling in frustration.

> **TROY**: (Cont'd)
> No way!

Just as he stops the clock clicks forward two minutes to 3pm.

> **AALIYAH:** (coming to a stop)
> All right, Troy, you did it.
>
> **TROY**: (raising his tired arms in victory)
> I won!

> **AALIYAH:** (hopping off her bike)
> You survived!

Rosa rushes over and hugs Troy around the waste.

> **ROSA**
> Mr. Troy, you did it! You did it!

Rosa steps back from him in disgust.

> **ROSA** (Cont'd)
> Eww. You're sweaty.

Troy stumbles around the exercise the room, to the floor. As he falls, the shakes his finger and gasps these words.

> **TROY**:
> 6pm, tonight, Rosa, you make sure your momma's ready. I'll be outside wafting for her.

Rosa and Aaliyah stand over the flattened out, fully exhausted Troy.

> **ROSA:**
> Is he alive?

> **AALIYAH:**
> I think so, Rosa.

EXT. AALIYAH'S HOME - NIGHT

Troy pulls up in his car. He gets out. He is well dressed but in a very conservative way, sweater vest, Corduroy pants etc.

Troy heads to the house and after a moment knocks on the door.

INT. AALIYAH'S HOME – NIGHT

Rosa answers the door to see Troy standing there.

> **ROSA:**
> Mr. Troy, you're alive!
>
> **TROY**:
> That's right, Rosa. Good as new.
>
> **ROSA:**
> How'd you like your workout today?
>
> **TROY:**
> Oh, you know me. Mr. Cardio.

Aaliyah appears at the top of the stairs. She is a vision but is dressed more in a fashionable little black dress, as if going out to a fancy dinner.

Troy looks up to the top of the staircase.

> **TROY**: (Cont'd)
> Oh. My. Goodness.

Rosa looks up.

> **ROSA:**
> Oh, mommy, you look like a princess.
>
> **TROY**:
> Indeed. Fantastic, Aaliyah, fantastic.

Aaliyah does a twirl at the top of the stairs.

> **AALIYAH:**
> Just a little somethin', I picked out.

Aaliyah comes down the stairs to see Troy. She looks him over.

> **AALIYAH:** (Cont'd)
> Oh, am I overdressed? Or are you 'underdressed?' I thought you said we were going 'downtown'?
>
> **TROY**:
> Uh, well, sort of. I mean, we are going downtown but...

Rosa interjects.

> **ROSA:**
> I'm going to see what Aunty is cooking for dinner!

Monica's voice comes booming from the kitchen.

> **MONICA:** (O.S.)
> Macaroni and cheese, like I told you!

Rosa exits.

> **TROY**:
> Hey, your sister's here. Why isn't she coming out to say 'hi'?
>
> **AALIYAH:**
> She thinks you'd be mad at her for setting you up in the poetry thing -
>
> **TROY**:
> Oh, that's right, I am mad.
>
> **MONICA:** (O.S.)
> Sorry, Troy, a meddling sister's gotta get her fun somehow!

TROY: (yelling back)
Well, all is forgiven, it will give me an opportunity to explore a new adventure!

MONICA (O.S.)
You a bad ass, Troy!

Troy stands there with a smile.

AALIYAH: (deadpan)
You two done?

TROY:
Guess so.

AALIYAH:
Now, where are we going, Troy?

INT. CHURCH COMMUNITY ROOM - NIGHT

Aaliyah, still in her glamourous outfit, and Troy, still in his sweater and Corduroy, sit on a couch together.

We pull back to see a room full of about Ten People, all casually dressed, seated, most with a Bible in their hands.

Aaliyah does not have one herself. Troy is holding a Bible.

Aaliyah clearly seems to be a bit out of place and uncomfortable.

Reverend Ron, about 60, speaks to the group.

REVEREND RON:
Well, Troy, I sure am glad you brought a guest with you to our Singles small group here tonight.

TROY:
Well, thank you, Reverend Ron. My friend here wanted me to choose an evening for us to enjoy, as friends, and I wanted to share with her the goodness and grace of my peoples.

REVEREND RON:
Well, many a marriage castle was built on the friendship foundation. Perhaps one day, you two won't be coming to our Singles Small Group together.

Almost everyone present nods and claps a little, while some utter words of encouragement to back the Reverend up. Edith and Margaret, two middle aged ladies, are the most vocal of everyone.

EDITH:
Praise Jesus!

MARGARET:
Lord, bless these children!

Everyone is very outwardly welcoming to Aaliyah except Betty Lynn, about 40, who eyes Aaliyah in jealousy, as Betty Lynn herself has a crush on Troy.

Aaliyah notices Betty Lynn giving her the evil eye and rolls her eyes away to avoid the harsh glance.

REVEREND RON:
Young lady, I know that our opening
45-minute Bible meditation was new to you, but I hope you did find it somehow *inspirational*.

AALIYAH: (trying to fit in)
Oh, yes. Very.

REVEREND RON:
Now, as is customary, young lady, towards the end of our bi-weekly meeting, I tend to say a few words.

Reverend Ron continues to talk as he seamlessly seg-ways into his sermon that he delivers from the front of the room.
Everyone turns their attention to Ron.

REVEREND RON: (Cont'd)
And it's unfortunate, that on my way here tonight... I passed by a homeless man. But it got me thinking... technically, we are all homeless. At one time, we have all felt hurt, lost, hopeless, had some addictions, or abused substances, things, and people. We have to check ourselves before we talk about somebody else. It takes a community to rise up and care for each other in our neighborhoods!

It's our responsibility to care for those that need rehabilitation and healing! Anything is possible with God! We are His vessels. We are created to do good works and show His glory to the world! If we say we love God, we must love our neighbors. We should be about our Father's business.

His ministry is tending to His flock and caring for His sheep. We are empowered by His Word to go out and teach all nations the Gospel! People are suffering and are in need of Christ. If you don't have anything to give anyone, you can give them hope by praying for them. We need each other because are one body in Christ! I love you all, my brothers and sisters!

The room erupts into a round of applause.

> **EDITH:**
> Yes, praise Jesus!

> **MARGARET:**
> Hallelujah!

Reverend Ron raises a hand to accept the applause before speaking again.

> **REVEREND RON:**
> Everyone, as most of you know, at the end of every Singles group, we bring up a different member of our group to say a few encouraging words to everyone. Now, y'all, a little birdie told me that one of you had something on their mind that they wanted to share tonight with our group. And now, I can see why. So, right now, I want to bring up one of our Singles Small Group members who has never spoken up here before. Troy Wilson, tonight is your night.

Reverend Ron extends his arm out.

Troy looks to Aaliyah on the couch.

Reverend Ron waves Troy to come up.

> **REVEREND RON:** (Cont'd)
> C'mon, Troy, don't get tight on me, now.

Troy gets up and goes to the front of the room.

> **TROY:**
> All right, y'all. I've been coming to this group for

two years but… it never struck me to actually speak up before. Until now. I guess I've been a little shy.

The room claps a little and calls out well wishes.

> **RANDOM SINGLE:**
> You got this, Troy!
>
> **EDITH:**
> Let it out, baby!
>
> **MARGARET:**
> C'mon, now!

Troy's POV: Troy looks over everyone in the room. His eyes cross over Betty Lynn, she gives Troy her best attentive smile.

But Troy's eyeline locks on Aaliyah, still alone in her cocktail dress, on the couch.

> **TROY**:
> When you hear the word love, what does it say to you? Now listen carefully to the sound of its pulse. It echoes the sweetness that pours out from our ears like honey. Love is an essential part of our daily nutrition. Without it, we wouldn't survive. Like the endless supply of air that we breath, we all thrive on the power of love.

Troy points to a cross on the wall.

The Single Group members nod in agreement and pay close attention.

> **TROY**: (Cont'd)
> The Creator of heaven and earth loved us so much, that He gave His first and last breath for us so that

> we could all have everlasting life. He died on a cross so that we may all have salvation. We meant so much to Him that He paid the ultimate price.

Still on the couch, now by herself **AALIYAH:** looks around the room puzzled.

> **TROY**: (Cont'd)
> Although we are sinners, through His eyes He loves us unconditionally.

Troy surveys the room and lands his eyes directly on Aaliyah again.

> **TROY**: (Cont'd)
> So what does it mean to love someone?

Betty Lynn stands up in a huff and excuses herself from the room with intent, the doors slam behind her as she exits.

Aaliyah notices Betty Lynn's harsh action but Troy is oblivious.

> **TROY**: (Cont'd)
> Take a moment to pay attention and you can see we have the perfect example to follow. Give willingly of yourself to someone you truly love. There is no profit to gain from love, only the serviceable act of charity...and that everyone, is what it means to love someone!

The room erupts in claps and "Amens."

> **REVEREND RON:**
> The Holy Spirit is alive in this brother!

> **MARGARET:**
> Oh my Lord, ewww child!

EDITH: (to Aaliyah)
Girl, you better rope him in before someone else does!

AALIYAH: (responding to Edith)
I'll keep that in mind.

Aaliyah looks to the front of the room where Troy basks in the limelight.

INT. TROY'S CAR – NIGHT

Troy drives, Aaliyah in shotgun.

AALIYAH:
Damn, where's that side of Troy been at this entire time?

TROY:
It's always been here, you just haven't discovered it yet.

AALIYAH:
Oh, I see.

TROY:
Perhaps, you inspired me with your lovely presence.

AALIYAH:
Hmmm...what about that Betty Lynn girl? She seemed a little *present*?

TROY:
Betty Lynn? That old cat lady? She's been single since the first Aunt Viv.

AALIYAH: (while laughing)
Well, see seemed a little put out by my lovely presence.

TROY:
Well, the Singles Group isn't used to dresses slammin' like that.

AALIYAH:
Well, the night's still young and this dress is too sexy to go home early.

Troy smiles and takes the next exit off the highway.

EXT. FRIENDSHIP FOUNTAIN – NIGHT

Troy and Aaliyah enter the area which is well lit with lights and a waterfall fountain.

AALIYAH:
Oh my God, this is where I would come to as a little girl. My daddy would take me here.

Aaliyah starts to tear up, Troy comes over to her and puts an arm around her shoulder asks her with his eyes, 'What's wrong, girl'?

AALIYAH: (Cont'd…while sniffling)
This was me and my daddy's spot. He was driving to pick me up from cheerleader practice after working the third shift. I knew he was tired, I knew it. He even asked me to get a ride home from someone else on the team but I didn't want to do that, I insisted that he pick me up. I was too ashamed that I didn't have my own car already and I didn't wanna ask anybody else but him. I was so

selfish. And my dad... was so tired. I cost my daddy his life.

Troy stands there soaking this in.

TROY:
Being a teenager is tough for everybody. The peer pressure? The cliques? It's all horrible.

TROY: (Cont'd)
If your daddy was here, I'm sure he would want you to enjoy your life. You've got a beautiful daughter and you've got your own business. You and your sister own a house together. I'm sure your father would be very proud and he would tell you that it was just an accident.

Aaliyah melts into Troy's chest, sobbing.

Troy consoles and holds her close.

AALIYAH:
You're a good friend, Troy. And you're a good man.

INT. TROY'S CAR - NIGHT

Troy drives with Aaliyah in shotgun looking out her window as the sights of Jacksonville pass.

A song on the radio plays to match their mood. Aaliyah turns the radio volume down.

TROY:
Hey, now. I was getting my groove on.

AALIYAH:
But what about you?

TROY:
What about me?

AALIYAH:
What's your problem?

TROY:
My what?

AALIYAH:
Your issue? I just spilled my guts to you out there. You know about me; single mom with the 'sort of on, sort of off' ex and the meddling sister. But what's your deal, Troy? What's your fatal flaw?

TROY:
Fatal flaw?

AALIYAH:
Everybody's got one. An Achille's Heel that makes them less than perfect.

TROY:
I'm just like everybody else. Just trying to get by.

AALIYAH:
Mud. I'm looking for mud, Troy. Get dirty for me.

TROY:
Huh. Okay. Well... you know, right now I don't have a job. But I'm, I'm working on that. I've got an interview scheduled.

AALIYAH:
For what?

TROY:
To be a cook. New Bar-B-Q place 'cross town. As long as this new 'Carolina Virus' doesn't kill us first.

AALIYAH:
What?

TROY:
A viral flu in China that's killin' people. My boss-to-be got it messed up and called it the 'Carolina Virus'. It's really just the most recent strand of Coronavirus; but it shouldn't get over here. We should be fine.

AALIYAH:
My God.

TROY:
Don't worry about it. Ol' Troy will take care of it.

AALIYAH:
No.

TROY:
No?

AALIYAH:
Don't change the subject. Achille's heel, Troy.

TROY:
Man. You're tough.

AALIYAH:
Yeah. I am. Don't leave me hanging. What's your problem?

TROY:
I don't have a problem.

AALIYAH: (freaking out)
Everybody's got a problem, Troy! *Everybody's* got problems! This is why you can't get intimate with me, Brett, you can't let your guard down!

Troy almost loses control of the car and it swerves a bit.

AALIYAH: (Cont'd)
Watch the fuckin' road!

TROY:
Yo, whoa, hold up with that Brett shit.

AALIYAH:
This ain't about Brett!

TROY:
You just called me his name. For the second time.

AALIYAH: (with attitude)
No, I didn't.

TROY: (mocking her voice)
Yes, you did. And that shit's getting old.

AALIYAH:
Okay, maybe I did. You're just like him. Hot and cold. Hot to the touch but cold on the inside.

TROY:
Yo, fuck that shit. I don't even know this guy.

AALIYAH:
Take me home.

TROY:
That's the plan.

They drive on.

SOUNDTRACK: Troy clicks on the music again.

They listen to a hard-hitting song for a while.

Aaliyah turns the station, much to Troy's annoyance. She finds a song that has lyrics that matches HER mood.

AALIYAH:
Troy. Just listen. Just listen.

Troy listens for a while, letting the song soak in.

Troy nods his head, letting Aaliyah's choice of song play without interruption.

They continue to listen as they drive on.

EXT. AALIYAH:'S HOME - NIGHT

Troy pulls up to her house. Troy zones out for a moment. Aaliyah looks to him.

AALIYAH:
Troy? Troy?

CU on Troy, closer and closer on his face. Finally, Troy speaks up.

> **TROY**:
> When I was in the military, I saw a few of my friends die. More than a few. Enough so you get used to it. You get used to it and then you know it's you. It's you next. Your day might come. You start to look forward to it.
>
> You start to wonder who will miss you, when you're dead. When you get killed. Who will take your flag.
>
> But then? When it doesn't happen, when you just go home, and you live on. A part of you wishes. You were dead.

Troy snaps out of his trance and realizes he's been speaking out loud.

Troy looks to his driving wheel.

Then he realizes, he's sitting in his car by himself.

INT. TROY'S CAR / EXT. TROY'S APARTMENT – NIGHT

Troy now fully realizes he's outside his own home. He has no memory of driving himself home after dropping off Aaliyah or how much he spoke to her.

Troy exits the car, in confusion, with a glazed look over his face.

He walks the stairs and enters his lonely apartment.

INT. TROY'S KITCHEN - NIGHT

Troy turns on the light and goes into the kitchen.
He sits in his kitchen chair. He pulls out his phone from his pocket to check if Aaliyah called or texted him to see if he's okay.
She did not.

Troy looks around his kitchen, stares at the light overhead.

A bug is dying in it, twitching in its final movements of life.

INT. TROY'S BEDROOM – NIGHT

Troy enters his bedroom and flicks on the light.

He sees his bed, with no sheets or blankets on it.

Troy looks around his meek surroundings.

He screams in guttural pain.

INT. VFW HALL BASEMENT – NIGHT

Troy sits in the circle with Pat, Eric and Craig. Everyone sits in an odd silence. There's now two empty chairs.

> **PAT:**
> Okay group, we're already running ten minutes late. It's unlike Caroline not to be here, she's been at every one of our meetings, ten minutes early, since I started leading this group four years ago. She respond to your text, Craig?

Craig checks his phone.

CRAIG:
No. Not as of now.

PAT:
We're just gonna have to start. Okay, guys, phone's off. We're just gonna have to focus.

Craig reluctantly puts his phone in his jacket pocket.

ERIC:
It's unusual to have two empty chairs.

PAT:
And why do we have even one empty chair, Eric?

ERIC:
The empty chair --

TROY: (taking over Eric's answer by force, as if in a trance) -- represents the Missing Solider. Or the Unknown Solider. The POW. Prisoner of War. The MIA. Missing in Action. Whatever you want to call him - or her - that has not made it home. In some sense, none of us have fully made it home.

Troy looks to a wall.

Right under the American Flag, is a POW/MIA flag.

PAT:
Have a good week, Troy? Any luck with that girl?

Troy just sneers back a look to Pat.

The tension is broken up by a buzz from Craig's phone.

PAT: (Cont'd)
Meeting's officially started, Craig. I'll again ask politely for phone's off.

CRAIG:
Right.

Craig pulls out his phone to turn it off but instinctively checks it out first.

CRAIG: (Cont'd)
I missed a call from Caroline. Should I call her back?

PAT: (looks at his watch)
Uh, it's against the rules.

ERIC:
Please, Pat.

PAT:
Yeah, fine, go ahead.

Craig excuses himself from the circle and takes his phone with him to a corner of the room to call back Caroline.

Meanwhile, Pat, Eric and Troy continue the conversation.

PAT: (Cont'd)
Troy, you were telling us at a previous about meeting a new lady in your life. Would you like to share how that's going?

TROY:
No. I got something else.

PAT:
What's that?

TROY:
Time lapses. Like when I was drinking.

PAT:
Are you drinking again, Troy?

TROY:
No. *When* I was drinking. That's the scary thing. Just the lapses. Without the drinking.

From the corner of the room, a scream is heard.

CRAIG:
NOOOOO!!

Everyone turns over to see Craig. His face is in shock.

Pat and Eric get up and go over to Craig, who's about fifteen feet from the circle.

ERIC:
What is it?

PAT:
What's wrong, Craig?

Troy looks over to them but stays in his chair.

CRAIG:
She's gone...

PAT:
What?

ERIC:
Caroline?!

CRAIG: (breathing heavy, in shock)
He, he killed her. Her ex... killed her. Her sister just told me.

Craig shoves his phone into Pat's hand.
Eric grabs an almost hysterical Craig tight while Pat takes Craig's smart phone and begins speaking into it.

PAT: (panicked, into the phone)
Hello? Hello? Is this true?

From his seat, Troy looks directly across from himself.

To two empty chairs.

As the others in the room continue with screams, cries and growing hysterics, Troy just stands up and walks out.

EXT. JACKSONVILLE - NIGHT INTO DAWN

Troy drives around town, listening to MUSIC to match his mood as he drives throughout the town with a glossed-over face.

He keeps driving until night gives way to day.

INT. CLUB EXPRESSIONS - NIGHT

Monica is on stage with the microphone.

MONICA: (in mic)
All right, House, we're just about ready for our wildcard round and we've got eight great new poets

here tonight. Well, actually, we've got seven... one of our newbies hasn't checked in as of now.

A Random Audience member yells out.

RANDOM AUDIENCE MEMBER:
Yo, what if he doesn't show up?

Monica looks to the side of the stage where she sees Aaliyah. They share a moment of uncomfortable eye contact.

MONICA: (in mic)
All right, chill y'all. The rule is a poet is not disqualified as long as they are here up on stage when their name is called.

Another angry voice is heard.

RANDOM AUDIENCE MEMBER # 2
Disqualify him NOW!

MONICA:
Damn, y'all is red-assed tonight. If he doesn't show up? I'll take that spot. And you know I can throw down.

The Audience applauds.

MONICA: (Cont'd...in mic)
Okay, House, first up in our sacrificial lamb first poet of the night spot, now no nepotism involved, in her long awaited return to the Club Expressions stage after a lengthy lay-off, a girl so beautiful, so fine, she must have a wonderful 'slightly' older sister to teach her everything about health and wellness... give it up for our girl Aaliyah.

Aaliyah comes onto stage and Monica backs off the microphone to allow Aaliyah to have it.

> **AALIYAH:** (into mic)
> Beaches and oceans, waves crash hard. When I got lost in your beautiful eyes, I forgot for a moment who I was and just wanted to swim into your eyes into a new ocean. But now... I feel like I'm in hell because of the pain and torture I've caused you. When you're hurting, I feel it. That closed door you hide behind? I can still hear your screams. Treading mud all over the carpet is like wiping your feet on someone's heart as if it were a doormat. And my shoes are dirty, soiled. How much lower will I go? I hate the way that I am and I hate the way I lie. I apologize for every tear that you've shed, for every road that I lead you down that turned out to be a dead end. I wanted to be friends but friends don't hurt friends. I hate the way I feel because feeling this way reveals my nature. My sad habit to destroy when I intend to create.

From the shadows of the room, a pair of eyes, covered from the shadows of a bookcase in the club, watches Aaliyah perform.

We would assume this to be Troy but later it's revealed to be someone else, just as interested.

Aaliyah lowers her head to signify she is done, and Monica comes back onto stage.

> **MONICA:** (in mic)
> All right, girl, you are good. Talent must run in your family. Now, if you thought that was good? We got a whole lot more in the Wild Card round tonight!

MONTAGE of the field of WILDCARD CONTESTANTS. (In editing, these poems can be cut down for time purposes).

Sexy Karen, 27, a hippy white chick, takes the stage and has a sex kitten mixed with punk rock delivery.

> **SEXY KAREN:** (in mic)
> Dogs and cats, cats and dogs. It's so sad to treat the one you love like a dog that you kick when you're in a bad mood. How can you expect the person you love to just roll over and pretend to play dead?

Sexy Karen's poem is interrupted by a GOOFY AUDIENCE MEMBER.

> **GOOFY AUDIENCE MEMBER:**
> They ain't dead, they're just sick of yo' ass!

The Crowd erupts in laughter.

From the edge of the stage, Monica stands and points out the offending Goofy Audience Member and threatens to eject him.

> **MONICA:**
> Shut yo mouth, fool!

Beatrice The Witch Doctor, 50, Takes the Stage.

> **BEATRICE THE WITCH DOCTOR:** (in mic)
> Her name is Karma. Somehow she became my attraction and I had to be extra vigilant. Her cruel and malignant ways try to keep me twisted around her little finger! She hovers around me like a dark cloud. She hovers around me like a dark cloud...
> Okay, let me stop before I get myself into more trouble.

Beatrice shakes her medicine stick at the audience.

> **BEATRICE THE WITCH DOCTOR**: (Cont'd…in mic)
> Beware of Karma, she will definitely put a spell on you!

Next poet up as Keep It Real Eddie, 30, who suffers from a stammer in his speech, which gives his delivery a chillingly dramatic effect, comes on stage next.

> **KEEP IT REAL EDDIE:** (in mic)
> If I'm brutally honest, I'd tell you to go to hell…but surprisingly all I can do is wish you well. Some stay for a season and some you'll never see again. That's the way it goes…The Light of the world can be flickering so bright one minute, and the next all lights go out! Trying to cling on desperately for all hope, but I'm left with nothing but anger, tears, and pain. Now little does anyone know, I am stronger and more resilient than anyone will ever give me credit for. I am a force to be reckoned with. I could clapback, I could ruin you but I'm a different guy now. I'm a changed man that will change atmospheres. I am healed and I have found clarity. I pray for people like you!

Our old pal Heckler J is next, performing in a full-on Clown outfit, but with a surprisingly introspective poem.

> **HECKLER J:** (in mic)
> The tears of a clown, when there's no one around? But what about when the Clown is around? Do you dare to laugh at a clown? His oversized shoes. His make-up. His little car. Is this clown, one that you spit on? When all he wants to do is make you laugh and smile?

The Crowd gives a respectful, almost tearful, applause to Heckler J. Now, it's Apocalypse John's turn. Apocalypse John believes that everything is coming to an end.

> **APOCALYPSE JOHN:** (in mic)
> Somewhere hearts have been broken, lives left shattered in pieces. Everything appears to have fallen apart. We're scattered among the Earth like a puzzle. Some of us don't know we fit. Most of us know something is missing. Images are distorted like a kaleidoscope; where can we go to find clarity? Sometimes there is nothing to do but scream.

Positive Petey is up next, who is like a motivational speaker mixed with a white Urkel type.

Petey comes onto stage wearing a Tom Brady Tampa Bay Buccaneers Jersey and an old school leather football helmet. Positive Petey is booed by the Crowd on just his walk to the stage alone.

> **POSITIVE PETEY:** (in mic, trying way too hard to be 'hip' and 'accepted')
> There is no point in playing defense when you can be on offense! Got that Mighty O... it more than compensates for the D I bring! I'm dedicated to winning, that's why I be grinnin'!

The Crowd boos Petey with no mercy until he gets off stage.

Monica comes back on stage, trying to deescalate the situation.

> **MONICA:** (in mic)
> Alright, we've seen - and heard - seven of the dopest poets in our city but I guess somebody ain't comin'. So, uh, I guess –

Troy comes out of nowhere to take the stage.

> **TROY**: (while headed up the stage)
> I'm here. Y'all, I'm here.

Troy speaks loud enough, he doesn't even need to use the house mic.

> **TROY**: (Cont'd)
> And 'here' is some place I never thought I'd be. Dropping knowledge, learning some myself and feeling... 'emotions'. Feeling... something. A friend of mine died. But didn't die. Was killed. Dead. Way before her time. And who killed my friend? A love. A lover. And this is not... an allegory. A metaphor. A simile. This is real life. Real blood. Real death. But love? It can kill in a different way, a softer way. It can make you feel... unwanted. Exposed. Abused. But love? It can also make you feel... alive. You take your poems, you take your thoughts, you take your sharings of imaginations? They're great. All great. Freedom. Of expression. But when that bell tolls? That knife cuts? It doesn't matter. You're dead. Like my friend. So... make this life... mean something. While you have it. If you love, love. If you hate, hate. But whatever you do? Feel.

Troy leaves the stage. Audience responds.
Monica comes back onto stage.

> **MONICA:** (in mic)
> Alright, House, well as you know, tonight was our Challengers Playoff. We've had eight slammin' poets tonight, y'all, so I want you to all give it up for all of 'em! Bring the noise, y'all, let 'em hear your love!

The AUDIENCE erupts in applause.

> **MONICA:** (Cont'd…in mic)
> Now, folks, we've got two 'anonymous' judges up in amongst your dedicated crew at Club Expressions
>
> **MONICA:** (Cont'd..she looks knowingly over to Emo Bartender)
> and the two of us, uh, I mean the two of them, have already cast their votes. But that third vote? That's up to you. Each of and every one of y'all.

The Audience responds with a dramatic OOOH and AHHH.

> **MONICA:** (Cont'd…in mic)
> Now, I'm gonna put a hand over each poet and when I do, I want you to make as much - or as little - noise as you want to for that particular poet. So, if it's someone you loved tonight, whoop it up. If it's someone who didn't quite fit your fancy, then silence is golden. You dig?

Audience responds as one collective voice, having been through this before as previous poetry slams.

> **AUDIENCE:** (together)
> We dig!
>
> **MONICA:**
> Okay, first up, we had Aaliyah.

Aaliyah takes a few steps forward and Monica puts a hand over her sister's head.

Audience ERUPTS well.

> **MONICA:** (Cont'd…in mic)
> I said, we had 'the beautiful, the talented, Aaliyah.'

Aaliyah blows a playful kiss to the crowd.

Troy watches her do this with a bit of judgement in his eyes. Aaliyah takes her place back in line.

Aaliyah and Troy have a terse stare down at each other.

Meanwhile, Monica takes the mic off the stand and takes it with her as she goes through the other contestants, putting her hand over each one's head as she says their respective names to get the Crowd reaction.

> **MONICA:** (Cont'd…in mic)
> Okay, y'all, how about, Beatrice the Witch Doctor? Heckler J? Keep it Real Eddie? Apocalypse John?

The crowd applauds respectfully enough for all of them.

> **MONICA:** (Cont'd…in mic)
> Sexy Karen?

The crowd boos Sexy Karen.

> **MONICA:** (Cont'd)
> What about?

Monica looks for Positive Petey but he's nowhere to be seen. The field of remaining poets all get back in line.

The crowds keep applauding with genuine affection.

> **MONICA:** (Cont'd…in mic)
> And finally, our late-comer, our rookie... how do you all feel about Military Man Troy?

Crowd applauds with genuine love for Troy, a feeling Troy has not felt in years.

Troy stands there on stage along with the other poets and his hard facial expression softens a bit.

As the cheers continue, Troy's eyes well up a bit. He touches his own welled up eye with his index finger, then brings the finger down to his own chest level. He studies the singular tear that's landed on the tip of his finger.

F/X: Through the filter of his own teardrop, Troy has a FLASHBACK to many of the intense moments he's experienced through the past few weeks; his relationship with Aaliyah, driving around Jacksonville, the loss of Caroline, etc.

As Monica goes through the following announcement, we focus on Troy and his fixation on the tear of his finger. He barely hears Monica.

> **MONICA:** (Cont'd...in mic)
> Okay, folks, now I've done all the tabulations between the crowd vote and the club votes.
>
> And talk about hard choices. Beatrice, Fast Eddie, Sexy Karen, Apocalypse John, please step up.

Beatrice, Fast Eddie, Sexy Karen and John all go step up to the front of the stage to face the Crowd.

> **MONICA:** (Cont'd...in mic)
> All four of you did great. But this was not your year. I'm sorry. Positive Pete, this goes for you too, wherever you are. The five of you did not make it to the Championship round next week. Step down, y'all. But please... come back.

The four of them accept another round of applause then step off the stage.

This leaves just Monica, Aaliyah, Heckler J, and Troy on stage.

As Monica says this upcoming part of her announcement, Troy wakes up out of his dream state to rejoin reality.

> **MONICA**: (Cont'd...in mic)
> Okay, y'all, that means, yes. These three poets will be the triad of contenders to challenge Brett Harris next week for the Voice of Jacksonville Championship next week. So, yes, with the tears of a clown when there ain't no one around, we've got Heckler J.

The Audience cheers.

Heckler J takes a bow to the crowd.

> **MONICA:** (Cont'd...in mic)
> And... We've got Aaliyah.

Aaliyah, with tears in her own eyes, waves to the crowd.

From the audience, we again see the EYES in the SHADOWS, watching Aaliyah intently from a distance. Now, we know these eyes don't belong to Troy because Troy himself is on stage.

> **MONICA:** (Cont'd...in mic)
> And...

Suddenly, Monica's microphone is swiped into the hand of a man.

The man is dressed in funky clothing, a jean jacket with patches all over it, and sunglasses with a well coifed hairstyle.

It's the man from the shadows of the club.

It's Brett.

> **BRETT**: (in mic)
> Wow! What a group of worthy contenders to my crown, y'all. You know, I'm gettin' a little shakey, I just might not show up next week.

A Random Brett Fangirl calls out from the audience.

> **BRETT FANGIRL:**
> Brett Harris! You're here!

She nearly swoons from her excitement.

Back to Brett, bogarting the stage.

> **BRETT:** (in mic)
> That's right, y'all, I am here. And I'll be here next week to take on...

Brett looks over his competition as Monica tries in vain to get her microphone back. Monica and Aaliyah exchange sisterly looks of "WTF" regarding Brett's unplanned Kanye-Taylor-esque taking over of the moment.

> **BRETT:** (Cont'd...(in mic)
> This wild cat, Freckles K!

> **HECKLER J:**
> That's Heckler J, sir, Heckler J!

> **BRETT:** (in mic)
> Yeah, whatever, you got it. Heckler JJ, DY-NO-MITE, next week, I'll see you then, and you can tell

the staff at your halfway house that you need a night pass.

Heckler J leaves the stage in a huff.

> **BRETT:** (Cont'd…in mic)
> And then, yes sir, yes sir, we got a little lady, who I know quite a bit about, much more than most of y'all. Aaliyah, girl, you sure you want some of this? I mean, more of it?

Aaliyah just stands there with a "FU" glare at Brett.

> **BRETT:** (Cont'd…in mic)
> Ew, damn, sorry folks, I think I've upset the little lady, once again. Hey girl, why you done go competing against the man for?

Aaliyah stands there, then her face gets full of rage and she goes on full on Angry Black Woman mode.

> **AALIYAH:**
> Why you gotta ruin everything, Brett?

> **BRETT:** (in mic)
> Hey, babe, it's show business, it's show business. And then finally, next week, I got this new brother we all saw tonight, now what was your name, son? Terry? Tyrese?

Troy stands stiff with eyes locked on Brett.

> **BRETT:** (Cont'd…in mic)
> Teddy? Tony? 'Ay yo, Tony Montana'? Whom I dealing with over here, brah? You speak or what?

Troy steps up to Brett, feeling the instinct to punch him in his face.

CU on Troy's hand as it clenches into a fist.

Aaliyah steps in front of Troy while Monica gets in front of Brett to separate them.

A terse stare down between Troy and Brett over the heads of the two sisters as the audience reacts. Brett lowers his sunglasses to see Aaliyah's close interaction with Troy.

Finally, Monica grabs the microphone from Brett.

> **MONICA:** (in mic)
> Ladies and gentlemen, here he is, the returning champion Brett Harris. He will be here next week for our Championship Voice of Jacksonville round. So don't you dare miss it.

INT. SALON – DAY

Aaliyah and Monica sit next to each other, getting their nails done at the same time by two SALON WORKERS.

> **AALIYAH:**
> Girl, the nerve of Brett --
>
> **MONICA:**
> Making a scene like that!
>
> **AALIYAH:**
> After weeks of being away!
>
> **MONICA:**
> I can't believe that mofo had the audacity to just show up --

AALIYAH:
Out of nowhere!

MONICA and **AALIYAH** Together
Like he –

As they speak, Brett comes into the salon through the front door, with a big smile on his face, holding hands with little Rosa, who she has a new STUFFED ANIMAL in her hands and a DISNEY MINNIE MOUSE hat on her head.

MONICA and **AALIYAH:** TOGETHER (Cont'd)
Owns the place!

BRETT:
Hey there, my favorite two ladies on the East Coast!

ROSA:
Daddy!

BRETT:
Make that, my second and third favorite ladies. Right after my little Minnie Mouse over here!

Brett scoops up Rosa into his arms and gives her a spin.

MONICA: (not impressed)
Where you two been?

BRETT:
Just catching up with my little girl.

AALIYAH:
It's a school day, Brett. Don't tell me --

ROSA:
We got on all the good rides!

AALIYAH: (quickly getting enraged)
Oh, no, you didn't. Disney?! On a Thursday?

BRETT:
Hey, don't get hot. It was a field trip. A little father-daughter bonding.

AALIYAH:
I told you; you could take her to school, not out of school. What did her teacher say?

As Aaliyah and Brett begin to argue, Rosa retreats into Monica's arms, who tries to protect her niece from her parents' dispute.

BRETT:
Oh, that ol' battle ax? Well, you know, I guess you can just tell her that --

AALIYAH:
That ol' 'battle ax' was the teacher last year, Brett. Now, Rosa's got a male teacher. You're telling me you didn't even call him? You're gonna leave that to me too?

BRETT:
A male teacher, huh? That a good idea?

AALIYAH:
I don't make those choices, Brett. I can't be havin' Rosa miss days of school for Disney World.

BRETT:
Well, next time, I'll take her to Epcot instead. That one's all about the environment and shit.

AALIYAH:
No Epcot, no Snow White, no Tea Cups in a Small World after all, if it means takin her out of school again, Brett. That's what the weekends are for.

BRETT:
Uh, yeah, but it's cheaper during the weekdays. And less crowded!

Aaliyah just stands there, fuming.

Rosa begins to cry and bolts into the back of the salon.

BRETT: (Cont'd)
Now, look what you done.
MONICA: (shaking her head)
Look what you've done, Troy.

Monica goes after little Rosa.

Brett stands there, exasperated, as he watches Monica go to the back of the salon. VARIOUS CUSTOMERS and WORKERS eye over Aaliyah and Brett.

BRETT:
Sorry, y'all, just a little 'mommy and daddy' disagreement. Go back to your surgeries.

The Customers and Workers roll their eyes and shake their heads at Brett's remark then go back to their own business.

Aaliyah lets out a big breath of anger.

INT. SALON BATHROOM - DAY

Rosa is in the bathroom, crying into tissue paper. The door knocks and Monica enters.

Monica sees her niece crying.

Monica takes a knee in front of Rosa.

> **MONICA:**
> Rosa, I'm so sorry. Did you have fun today with your dad?
>
> **ROSA:**
> Yes, I did. Why does mommy have to yell?
>
> **MONICA:**
> She was just surprised. That bas-- Brett -- your dad - didn't tell us he was taking you to Orlando. We had no idea.
>
> **ROSA:**
> Is mommy mad at me?
>
> **MONICA:**
> No, honey, not at all. But, it's just... Brett -- your dad -- he's got to be a little bit better about being a full time dad not just a fun time dad. Your mom's been trying to get him to be like that... for years. But I... I don't know if it's in him. Maybe we should just accept your daddy for what he is.

Rosa takes the hat off her head to show her aunt.

> **ROSA:**
> He bought me a hat.

> **MONICA:**
> It's nice.

> **ROSA:**
> If my daddy is not a good daddy, why doesn't mommy make Mr. Troy my daddy?

Monica just looks at her niece, speechless.

INT. SALON - DAY

Aaliyah and Brett have now moved over to a more private area of the salon and are seated in a deeper state of conversation.

> **AALIYAH:** (messing up his name)
> Troy, you know Rosa loves you, but I can't just have you just coming into town and taking Rosa out of school like this without even telling me. That undermines me as her mother.

> **BRETT:** (half mouthing this)
> 'Troy?'

Aaliyah ignores his 'Troy' response as if she doesn't even hear it or realize that she called him by Troy's name.

> **AALIYAH:**
> Field trips are cute but they don't make a dad.

> **BRETT:**
> More than my dad ever did.

Aaliyah takes Brett's hand into her own.

AALIYAH:

Please, I've told you this. I can't be 'bad cop' all the time.

BRETT:

No one's asking you to be. But I got to spend time with my girl.

AALIYAH:

Spend time doing homework. Spend time having dinner. Disney's the cheap way to her heart and you know it.

BRETT:

I should have asked you to go. I know it. Next time.

AALIYAH:

On a Thursday, her ass needs to be in school. Not on Pink Elephants.

BRETT:

We went to the Presidents show. Those President robots are amazing. Very educational.

AALIYAH:

Look, Brett, how long you been gone? Five weeks? Six?

BRETT:

Four but who's counting?

AALIYAH:

And I'm sure since last we've met, you've had some 'fun on the road'. And that's fine. But look, you can't come up in here and just swoop in like you own Jacksonville and then go back on tour like Prince and do whatever you please. You'll always be Rosa's dad. But I got needs too. And I can't be…

BRETT:
Needs? Woman, I'm trying to make this work for both of us --

AALIYAH:
There's no money in poetry, Brett. So, let's put that dream to rest.

BRETT:
Hey, yo --

AALIYAH:
Those ten-dollar books you sell out of your car are just enough for gas from one hoochie to the other. They ain't doing shit for me and Rosa.

BRETT:
Yo, I sense some hostility.

AALIYAH:
And that fucking sideshow last night? You stole the moment from me and the other poets.

BRETT:
Mmm. What about that? I thought my people would be happy to see. Build things up for next week. I was surprised to see you up on stage, challenging me.

AALIYAH:
It wasn't fair, Brett. The club has grown. It's got more voices than just yours now.

BRETT:
I see. I see you. And I hear you.

AALIYAH:
Oh. You do, huh?

BRETT:
What was up with that freak last night?

AALIYAH:
Heckler J?

BRETT:
No. Not the clown. The other one. The ex-con.

AALIYAH:
Ex-con? Who you talkin' 'bout?

BRETT:
The 'Military Man'. Terrance. Tyrone. Whatever the fuck his name is, guy's got a weird vibe to him. That two-thousand-yard stare.

AALIYAH:
Troy? He's fine.

BRETT:
How 'fine' do you think he is?

AALIYAH:
He's a friend. That's it. Let it go.

BRETT:
Mmm?

Aaliyah stands, leaving Brett seated by himself.

AALIYAH:
Twelve years, one child and zero ring. Change the math on that and we change the tone of this conversation.

Brett folds up in his chair.

AALIYAH: (Cont'd)
Until then? You're out of your question allotment for today. 'Git.

Aaliyah extends her thumb to show Brett the door.

BRETT:
What about tomorrow?

AALIYAH:
And tomorrow. The whole week.

Brett heads to the door to exit.

BRETT:
One of these days I just might surprise you, Ms. Aaliyah. Your ring finger still a size eight?

AALIYAH:
Eight and a half. Same size for twelve years, Mr. Brett. Until it wilts up and falls off my hand from old age.

They look at each other and share a hard-earned half-smile as Brett exits the salon.

Through the salon glass wall, Aaliyah watches Brett out on the street, go to his car and open up his trunk to organize his books of poetry.

Aaliyah shakes her head in resigned frustration.

> **AALIYAH:** (Cont'd...sadly, to herself)
> Dreamer. Ain't nothin' but a dreamer.

INT. VFW HALL - NIGHT

There is a large tribute photograph of Caroline and her years of living at the front of the room.

The gathering of mourners in the room take their seats.

Pat, the leader of the Veterans group, dressed in appropriate Military garb, goes to the front of the room at a podium.

> **PAT:**
> Family. Friends. Folks. We are gathered here under the saddest of circumstances. Our beloved friend Caroline, always outspoken herself, was silenced last week. But her words live on.

Pat leaves the podium.

Troy enters and takes the spot at the podium.

> **TROY:**
> 'Dear Soldier, from one veteran to another, I've been in your shoes. I know what it's like to be deployed to a combat zone in a foreign country. Who knows how long you will be gone?
>
> Six months? A year? Away from your family. You try to close the gap in distance by making phone calls and writing letters. You may feel like you're forgotten. But you're not. I have the utmost respect for you and what you do.

Hold on, good soldier. What you're experiencing right now will pass soon enough. Continue to focus on your mission. Be safe and keep your head on a swivel. Stay in the fight, your country loves you and need you, even when they don't say they do. I know we do. We love you. God is watching over you all.'

Troy takes a moment.

TROY: (Cont'd)
These are words published in the VFW Monthly newsletter, December issue, twelve years ago, from our departed sister, Corporate Sergeant Caroline Richter of the Third Armored Cavalry Regiment. I only met Caroline Richter a short time ago. I was in a coffee house and she noticed me opening mail from the service. She spoke to me and offered her opinions... on a lot of things.

Members of the Memorial Service GATHERING laugh knowingly.

TROY: (Cont'd)
In that first conversation, Ms. Caroline got a read on me pretty good. Like she knew me my whole life. It was scary. She was the person, the soldier, and the lady, who suggested I join the small group we have here twice a week.

She is the one who recognized this anger inside me and told me it was eating me up. Ms. Caroline was the one who cared enough to speak up to me and try to help when others just turned their heads from me in fear.

Troy leaves the podium.

The GUYS try to stop Troy to congratulate him for a well delivered speech.

But Troy just walks out.

EXT. JACKSONVILLE - DAY

Troy drives. Listening to music. Eyes glazed.

EXT. ST. AUGUSTINE CHURCH - DAY

Troy stands outside a church, just looking at it. He does not enter it. His car is still running with MUSIC coming from it.

INT. CHURCH COMMUNITY ROOM - NIGHT

The usual group exit the room after a meeting.

Reverend Ron cleans up the room by himself.

Troy waits for the others to fully exit and then enters on his own.

Reverend Ron turns to see Troy.

> **REVEREND RON:**
> Troy. My friend. We haven't seen you. You alright?

Troy shakes his head 'no'.

Reverend Ron leads Troy to take a seat in a pew.

> **REVEREND RON**: (Cont'd)
> What's wrong, son?

> **TROY**: (trembling)
> Just about everything.

Reverend Ron goes on Rev mode.

> **REVEREND RON:**
> You are the head and not the tail. You have the power and the dominion to trample over serpents and scorpions.

Troy listens.

> ### EXT. CLUB EXPRESSIONS - NIGHT

The outside of the club as a LINE OF PEOPLE begin to form.

> ### INT. CLUB EXPRESSIONS - NIGHT

INTERCUT: As Ron talks to Troy in the CHURCH, we begin to segway back and forth to a Flash Forward to the finals of the Poetry Competition being set up; the Crowd filling up CLUB EXPRESSIONS, Monica all dressed up as MC addressing the Crowd, etc.

To Ron and Troy in the CHURCH.

> **REVEREND RON:**
> God has put us on a new path and given us a new direction. Thank God for his wonderful protection.

Back to CLUB EXPRESSIONS. PRE-SHOW WARM UP

MONTAGE:

Troy, Aaliyah, Heckler J, and Brett all warm up in their own ways in separate little nooks and crannies of Club Expressions, getting ready for their final battle.

In a HALLWAY, Heckler J goes through his routine, practicing his performance.

Brett sits on a staircase, grooving out to MUSIC in his earbuds, while using the visualization technique of seeing himself in his mind on stage performing, playing his fingers in the air like he is conducting an orchestra.

We hear Reverend Ron's voice over the visuals of Club Expressions.

    REVEREND RON: (V.O.)
    We are in this World, but we are not of this World.

To Aaliyah in a dark corner of Club Expressions, pacing in nerves. Monica enters and the two sisters make deep eye contact with each other, then hug.

Back to Ron preaching to Troy in the Church.

    REVEREND RON:
    Man will fail you, but God never does, and he never will!

Troy listens.

To CLUB EXPRESSIONS. Troy stands in the back of the club, alone in a CROWD, watching Monica address the large Crowd, that is finally all taking their seats.

Troy's POV: He hears Monica speak to the Crowd but her voice is accompanied by a painful 'buzz' in his ear.

> **MONICA:** (in mic)
> House... we're here, y'all. We're here. And we've got four bad ass poets ready to take the stage for you tonight! So, let me hear your thunder and these poets are ready to bring the lightning.

To Reverend Ron in the CHURCH.

> **REVEREND RON:**
> Some of us are born with family we can depend on! Others, like you, young man, are brought into this world a lone wolf, who must hunt for his own food and seek his own adventure! The traveling wolf needs no comfort; his feet are his dwelling, the Earth his pillow.
>
> This lost son with no master...travel the world, young man, find yourself what you're looking for! God helps those that help himself; you want something in this world, you go out and get it!

INT. CLUB EXPRESSIONS – NIGHT

Troy still watches Monica on stage from his spot in the back of the club.

> **MONICA:** (in mic)
> Okay, now how this is gonna work is we got a two-round set up, y'all, semi-finals and finals. And guess what? Our defending champion has opted to go...first. That's right, here he is, straight back from his World Tour, and his unexpected appearance here last week, the one and only... Brett Harris!

From his spot, Troy tenses up as he sees Brett take the stage.

Brett gets a big round of CHEERS but also an undercurrent of boos from the CROWD.

> **BRETT:** (in mic)
> Oh, it's gonna be like that, y'all?

The Crowd moans.

> **BRETT:** (Cont'd...in mic)
> I am the defending Champion, you know. And I'm here to represent you. Now, let me tell you about the night, you almost lost me. Got me gassed up, foot on the gas pedal, I'm still coming for that velocity, coming with that ferocity, ain't with that mediocrity, can't be associated with that atrocity.
>
> All these years, I stayed in my lane, but one night it almost ended on Interstate 180. I'm curvin', then swervin', then flippin' in my Benz three times! That seatbelt came in handy, I came out like a dandy. Laid out in the Johnny Blaze fit, could went out in ablaze in that wreck!
>
> Blood on my Lugz, it was a cold night, mouth full of dirt, man it hurt. Crashed but didn't burn. I am a survivor.

Brett waits, expecting a huge applause from the Crowd but it doesn't come. Instead, a mediocre splattering of applause.

This gets in Brett's head.

> **BRETT**: (Cont'd...in mic)
> If I was brutally honest, I'd tell you all to go to

> hell... but surprisingly, all I can is wish you well. People come, people go. Some stay for the season, some stay for the trilogy. The world can be bright one moment and turn dark the next. I need to expose some things to the light. By no means, am I a perfect man...I make tons of mistakes. I've hurt and disappointed many people. But all of that doesn't define my true character. People often sleep on the good you do and your good qualities...

We go to Troy watching, from his spot in the back of the room.

Troy's POV: The buzz in his ears resumes, overpowering Brett's voice in the microphone.

Finally, Troy sees Brett leave the stage unceremoniously.

Troy then sees Monica introduce Aaliyah but at this point, the buzz in Troy's ear overwhelms Monica's voice from Troy's perspective.

> **MONICA:** (in mic)
> Oh, Lord, folks we gotta little family drama tonight. Just the luck of the draw, guess who is Brett Harris's opponent in the first round?

Familiar with the Brett-Aaliyah relationship, the Crowd "OOOHS" and "AHHHS" with interest and anticipation.

> **MONICA:** (Cont'd...in mic)
> That's right, House, here is... Aaliyah.

Aaliyah takes the stage.

Troy watches her from his spot in the back of the club.

Brett watches Aaliyah from the side of the stage.

Aaliyah can feel the weight of both of their stares.

>**AALIYAH:** (in mic)
>(she takes a deep breathe and closes her eyes)
>
>Even a Queen can feel remorse. Even a Queen can feel... Hate.

(she opens her eyes and picks up the pace)

>Hate the way I lie. When you're hurting, I hurt just as bad. How much lower will I go? I've waited my whole life for your entrance but the way you've treated me demands your exit, overdue like Brexit, an international incident with the weatherman saying 'inclement is imminent'. But this journey, this dual driven ship of fools, hopeless romantics in a panic, needs a respite. You're looking for something but I'm not it. My scene and my scenario, you gotta go.

(Beat, she begins to deliver in a softer, more apologetic tone.)

>I told you when you got on the Queen's bus, the riders serve the Queen not the other way around. Now you gotta go somewhere I can't take you. Keep ya head up but put your feet to the ground. I have faith you'll find your destination; the place you don't even know you need to be yet. It's waiting for you, but I can't take you. I can't go with. We had a good ride, but we're headed in different directions. We passed in the night at one of life's intersections. Don't make it painful, make it gainful, what did you learn from this experience?

Aaliyah looks to the side of the stage, where she sees Brett looking back at her.

Then she looks out into the crowd.

Where she sees Troy. Through the fog of the club, Aaliyah and Troy make eye contact and hold each other's stare for a moment.

Then Aaliyah looks back to Brett on the side of the stage, then back forward to the audience.

She closes her eyes again and delivers her poem's final line with a deadpan edge.

> **AALIYAH:** (Cont'd...in mic)
> You'd never guess... this poem...
> ain't.... about you.

Aaliyah leaves the stage. The Crowd Pops with awed applause.

From his position in the back of the club near the bar, Troy watches her exit, the ringing in his ears now starting to lower.

As Aaliyah exits the stage, Brett goes to embrace her but she walks right by him.

INT. CLUB EXPRESSIONS BACKSTAGE - NIGHT (CONTINOUS)

Aaliyah finds a private area backstage and holds herself, tears begin to stream down her face.

INT. CLUB EXPRESSIONS - NIGHT (CONTINOUS)

Monica goes to the microphone.

MONICA: (in mic)
All right, House, now it's time for your vote on our first semi-final.

Brett comes out on stage, waving to the crowd. He now carries a gaudy customized "VOICE OF JACKSONVILLE" Championship Wrestling Belt with him and is now wearing a crown on his head and even a cape.

BRETT:
I'm here, y'all, I'm here! Happy to defend my title!

MONICA: (in mic, looking over Brett's 'gimmicked' outfit)
Oh, my. Okay, where's Aaliyah? We need to take this vote.

BRETT:
Just let the people know, I'm advancing, Monica. Happy to move forward.

Monica looks around but Aaliyah is nowhere to be seen.

MONICA: (in mic)
Okay, folks, the bi-laws say we don't even need the poets on stage for this round of voting to be valid, just y'all's noise shall suffice.

BRETT:
Bi-laws?

MONICA: (in mic, mocking Brett)
Okay, Mista Harris, you can 'git yoself off my stage now, so I can take this here tally.

BRETT:
This is my stage.

> **MONICA:** (in mic, firm)
> No. This is *my* stage. Now git to steppin'.

Metaphorically castrated by his sister-in-law Monica, Brett exits. Monica eyes him as he leaves suspiciously and waits for him to be fully gone before she continues.

> **MONICA:** (Cont'd…in mic)
> All right, House, so who gives it up for our defending champion Brett Harris?

As if on cue, Brett comes out into the front of the crowd, not on the stage but into the spotlight just in front of the stage, where he raises an arm to the crowd with a Don King-esque con man's smile.

> **BRETT:** (to Crowd)
> Vote for me, y'all, defending Champ here, I'm doing you proud, worldwide!

The Crowd gives a large round of noise but a lot of boos are mixed with the spattering of positive energy cheers.

> **MONICA:** (in mic)
> Um… I see. All right, then, whaddya say, for one of challengers, our girl Aaliyah?

The Crowd erupts in mostly positive applause and cheers. Even a chant of 'Aaliyah' breaks out.

> **MONICA:** (Cont'd…in mic, genuinely stunned)
> Aw, shit. Our defending champion Brett Harris…

CU on Brett's smiling face as he looks out to the audience.

> **MONICA:** (O.S.) (Cont'd…in mic)
> Has been defeated…

Brett's face drops in humiliation. To Monica on stage.

> **MONICA:** (Cont'd…in mic)
> In the first round to our girl… Aaliyah…that was a bold choice, House.

Brett looks up to Monica from the floor.

> **BRETT:**
> That's some BS, I demand a recount!

> **MONICA:** (in mic)
> No, honey chil', that verdict is clear; Aaliyah is the winner, dear. That means Aaliyah will be facing the winner of our next semi-final matchup between our resident clown prince Heckler J and our Club Expressions newcomer 'Military Man' Troy.

Brett shakes his fists in rage.

> **BRETT:**
> I can't believe this conspiracy!

Now, unbalanced in defeat, Brett goes charging towards the back of the stage.

INT. CLUB EXPRESSIONS BACKSTAGE – NIGHT

Aaliyah has been listening to the announcements from backstage and her tears have dried and she now has a glow of hope and disbelief on her face.

Monica enters the area and finds Aaliyah.

AALIYAH:
I… beat Brett?

They look deep into each other's eyes with sisterly love.

MONICA:
You did, girl. You did.

Aaliyah smiles.

MONICA: (Cont'd)
But this thing ain't over. And your job ain't done.

INT. CLUB EXPRESSIONS - NIGHT

Back on stage, Heckler J now takes the microphone. Heckler J is now dressed in a corny "private school boy's outfit". The Crowd laughs at his outfit. Heckler waits for the crowd's laughs to die down.

HECKLER J: (in mic)
Inside every man is a little boy crying for attention. A little boy that is in pain and needs to be lifted up.

Although I'm no longer a child, I've grown into a man that still has the innocence of a child inside. Sometimes I just want to hide and be sheltered from this cold, cruel world. Most people are oblivious to their surroundings.

But if they see a child crying and they come running to the rescue. But when an adult man cries? His tears dry ignored. Am I still that child now in a man's suit? Begging for your attention?

INT. CLUB EXPRESSIONS BACKSTAGE - NIGHT

Brett enters the backstage area, looking for Aaliyah.

He finds her.

They immediately start arguing.

INT. CLUB EXPRESSIONS - NIGHT

Watching from the back of the club, Troy begins to feel Heckler J's words strike close to home.

> **HECKLER J:** (in mic)
> Or does this Court Jester have for you more than just jokes? Has a clown ever told you to pursue your goals in life, your ambitions, your happiness?

Troy leaves his spot and works his way through the crowd to the front of the room, during Heckler J's poem.

> **HECKLER J:** (O.S.) (Cont'd..in mic)
> Has a clown ever asked you to *love*?
> To *find love*? To fight for love?

Troy veers left into the backstage area.

INT. CLUB EXPRESSIONS BACKSTAGE - NIGHT (CONTINOUS)

Troy enters the backstage area.

He sees Aaliyah in her state of distress.

Troy moves closer forward to her, about to approach her.

But as Troy gets closer to Aaliyah, Brett comes into Troy's view.

From the front of the club, Monica's voice is heard.

> **MONICA:** (O.S.) (in mic)
> Thank you Heckler J. Our next - and final - challenger is our Military Man Troy.

Troy freezes in his tracks.

> **MONICA:** (O.S.) (Cont'd...in mic)
> TROY?

Brett sees Troy out of the corner of his eye, but does not acknowledge Troy and Troy does not realize Brett saw him.

Seeing Troy, Brett does a quick apology to Aaliyah to calm her down.

A master of manipulation, Brett gets a hug out of Aaliyah, just so Troy can see it.

As they hug, Brett takes a special glee in knowing Troy is watching this.

> **MONICA:** (O.S.) (Cont'd...in mic)
> Troy... going once?

Aaliyah is totally oblivious to Troy being in the area.

CU on Troy's face.

> **MONICA:** (O.S.) (Cont'd...in mic)
> Troy, don't do this to me now. Going twice...

Brett digs deeper into his hug on Aaliyah, then even gives her a kiss on the mouth to rub the salt deeper into Troy's wound.

Troy sees this, turns and exits the backstage area.

Aaliyah pushes away from Brett's kiss.

Brett smiles.

Aaliyah exits in a huff.

INT. CLUB EXPRESSIONS – NIGHT

Troy enters the stage, direct from the backstage scenario he just witnessed. A solemn expression takes over his face.

He immediately goes to the microphone and recites the poem he had prepared but, as if in a hypnotic state, the performance lacks genuine emotion.

> **TROY**: (in mic)
> I stand at the door and knock, waiting for God's response. He tells me to come forth. I enter His sanctuary and humble myself before His throne. I fall to my knees and bow before His Majesty. My tongue confesses my sins to be forgiven. I thank Him for all the blessing he's allowed me to receive.

Aaliyah comes rushing up to the side of the stage but freezes in her tracks in the wings as she sees Troy perform.

Troy hears Aaliyah and then twists his neck to see her standing there on the side of the stage.

Troy steps back from the microphone. Takes a deep breath. Then he steps back to the mic. Freestyles.

> **TROY**: (Cont'd…in mic)
> Can't believe I was a chump. Can't believe I believed in you, believed in us, believed in U.S., believed in anything. Can't believe I believed in my

country, in my people, in my family, in my friends. Can't believe this is how the story ends. A lone soldier, unknown soldier, finger on the pulse. Pull the trigger, out of my misery.

Troy sees Aaliyah watching him from the side of the stage, her eyes welling up with tears.

TROY: (Cont'd...in mic)
What was I fighting for?

Not for a guarantee but just a chance. At what? Wife and kid? Picket fence? Happiness? My true state of mind has no relief. Just disbelief. Some gave all, more than me, but I gave a lot. And it wasn't enough. Can't believe... I was a chump. At the end of the day, buses come and go, and it turns out, your destination was just another dead end I avoided. There will be another ride to hop on and off.

Another road less travelled I get lost on. Another adventure maybe I can make sense of, maybe I can't. Same old life lesson, no matter how many fairy tales reveal themselves as nightmares. On the final stage, there will be no crowd votes and no judges on my worth as a human being, a citizen, a soldier and a man. I am my own best friend.

Troy steps back from the microphone.

F/X: Slow/Mo: Aaliyah leaves her spot on the side of the stage and rushes to Troy but as she does, he's already mid-jump from the stage to the floor of Club Expressions.

From the stage, Aaliyah calls out to Troy as he makes his way through the Crowd of Poets and Freak Witnesses.

AALIYAH: (calling out)
Troy! Troy!

Monica holds back Aaliyah who's broken into sobs of anxiety. Troy exits Club Expressions, without waiting for the verdict.

EXT. CLUB EXPRESSIONS – NIGHT

Troy comes outside, immune to anyone around him.

He looks up to see a Full Moon shining down him and the city as the noise of the poet house begins to fade.

Troy looks down to the sidewalk where he sees a stray DOG facing him, with no collar, no leash, no tags, which looks like another wild lone wolf.

Troy and the canine have a moment of understanding.

CU on Troy's eyes and the wolf-dog's reflection in them.

FADE OUT.

THE END.

www.ingramcontent.com/pod-product-compliance
Lightning Source LLC
Chambersburg PA
CBHW071455070526
44578CB00001B/353